Essays
of a Penitentiary
Philosopher

Essays
of a Penitentiary
Philosopher

Phillip Torsrud

ESSAYS OF A PENITENTIARY PHILOSOPHER

iUniverse books may be ordered through booksellers or by contacting:

iUniverse
1663 Liberty Drive
Bloomington, IN 47403
www.iuniverse.com
1-800-Authors (1-800-288-4677)

Because of the dynamic nature of the Internet, any web addresses or links contained in this book may have changed since publication and may no longer be valid. The views expressed in this work are solely those of the author and do not necessarily reflect the views of the publisher, and the publisher hereby disclaims any responsibility for them.

The views expressed in this work are solely those of the author and do not necessarily reflect the views of the publisher, and the publisher hereby disclaims any responsibility for them

Any people depicted in stock imagery provided by Getty Images are models, and such images are being used for illustrative purposes only. Certain stock imagery © Getty Images.

ISBN: 978-0-5954-8518-5 (sc)
ISBN: 978-0-5956-0609-2 (e)

Print information available on the last page.

iUniverse rev. date: 05/03/2019

Contents

Part II

AUTHOR'S NOTE

This book is very critical of the government and politicians, especially in the manner in which they've addressed our nation's crime problem. If you believe our great leaders have already solved that problem, then this book is not for you. Our crime problem continues to have a deep impact on countless people across the nation and I feel compelled to tackle this complicated topic. One of the reasons for having freedom of speech is so that people outside of the mainstream, like me, can bring new ideas to the public debate on how to better our society. We remain open to all possibilities and all solutions. The experience of the criminal is one that is lacking in the debate on how we address crime and I hope that in my own small way I can correct that a bit.

Let no criminal think for one moment that my criticisms of the system are to be used as excuses or rationalizations as to why they have failed to abstain from criminal activities. We must look at ourselves first, regarding what changes need to be made, if we want to avoid repeating our mistakes. Every time a criminal gets out of prison and goes right back to committing crimes, they provide more ammunition to those factions opposed to rehabilitation and eager to empower the state with more money and more laws to lock criminals up and throw away the key. So, my first criticism regarding the system being what it is, must in all fairness go to those recidivist criminals who are such willing accomplices in their own destruction. Criminals show no "love" for their fellow convicts by continuously returning to prison as though it were a Holiday Inn. If criminals cared about themselves or each other, despite all the "brother" chatter, they would understand their responsibility upon release to show the world that we are not animals, that we can change, that there is hope, and most importantly that we are men.

Personally, I would not have the insight to understand and explain things the way I do without understanding where I've gone wrong. My experience allows me to see things from the standpoint of the criminal. Why should anyone care? If you are honest about trying to solve today's problems, you will want to see a different perspective. Where you stand does impact what you see as well as how you see it. A philosopher embraces all knowledge, regardless of the source, and that's why I use the title, Essays of a Penitentiary Philosopher. If you understand philosophy, you know that not only can philosophy come from a prison, but trying to address issues like crime without hearing from the prisoners reflects a desire to remain in a state of will-full ignorance.

While most of the essays in this book are about crime, I do touch on a few other important topics in the last couple essays. This gives you, the reader, a broader array of my method of thinking allowing you more points of reference to determine if my conclusions are plausible. Some will surely mock me for thinking of myself as a philosopher, but because I can see myself as a philosopher, I can also see everyone else having that potential. Hopefully, this book inspires people to realize their potential. This is the basis of all crime prevention.

PART I

"Jails and prisons are the complement of schools; so many less as you have of the latter, so many more you must have of the former."

Horace Mann

CULTURE

Culture is not just paintings, clothes, books and songs. This might come as a shock to those who feel they are highly cultured due to their knowledge or ownership of items that are products of our world's cultures. Some of those items can be quite costly. Is money necessary to become highly cultured? Where do culture and market meet, and what are the consequences? The commercialization of culture has played a large role in its degradation. The result is the valuation of the product over the experience, history and knowledge which led to that product's creation.

Culture is like jam, the less one has, the more one has to spread it about. If "cultural" products are being sold, culture will be spread out as thin as possible to make the greatest profit. This is reflected by how loosely the term culture is now used, thereby devaluing its currency to the point where it lacks any real meaning. Culture is beyond any material object, yet those objects can serve to reflect or express certain elements of a culture. Culture is more than the sum of its parts and that's what makes it so difficult to fully grasp. It provides the depth and substance from which societies find their spiritual nourishment. For the individual, culture is a way of experiencing life itself.

Realizing the magnitude of what culture provides is a prerequisite to addressing the cultural problems we face. Understanding that culture isn't a material product, allows us to seek beyond simple, material solutions. Think of how complicated a person's relationship can be with either their parents, spouse, or friends. Now combine a person's relationships throughout their life with religion, family, friends, media, government, education and work place, and that gives you an idea of a person's culture. Those institutions, which together comprise society, are what have taught that individual the norms and values that create the platform for their culture. My high school World Cultures teacher, Mrs. Bonesho, defined culture simply and eloquently as, "shared, learned behavior."

Newt Gingrich and his fellow Republicans used the slogan, "It's the culture, stupid!" to summarize what was wrong in America during the 1994 elections. Since rising crime rates were a big political issue, this strategy was very successful.

Republicans took over both House and Senate and were able to hold them until 2006. Throughout this period they used the "Culture War" issue effectively.

Republicans were right in that a behavioral problem, high crime rates, were a reflection of an ailing culture. Fixing that problem would not be easy, yet Republicans made it sound so simple. While getting tough on crime was not really a new solution, Republicans did take a renewed effort at an old idea that never worked. History is full of little ironies. The fact that Republicans could think of nothing better than doing exactly what the Communists did when they came to power is amazing. "In February, 1918, the Chairman of the Council of People's Commissars, Comrade Lenin, demanded that the number of places of imprisonment be increased and that repression of criminals be intensified." The communists planned to change their culture too.

Republicans will claim that this comparison is unfair, and more importantly, that their strategy has been successful. Their success can be backed by the decrease in crime throughout their reign, until around 2005 when crime rates began increasing again. This, they might claim, was a result of the criminals knowing Democrats would soon take back both Houses of Congress in 2006. Timing is everything in politics.

In 1973, the Supreme Court legalized abortion. As clinics opened and services became more available to the general public, the number of abortions increased. What that meant for the Republicans of 1994 was that the number of people between the ages of 16 and 25 would greatly decrease in the coming years. This demographic commits more crimes than any other. Based on simple math, the Republicans could have claimed that if Americans flossed their teeth every day, crime would go down, and it would have happened. On top of the good demographic picture, the economy did well for most of the time between 1994 and 2006. Demographics and economics are the key to keeping crime rates down, and America was fortunate for a while in that regard. That time has now passed and we are back to square one. While building lots of prisons, Republicans have failed to change the culture one bit.

All any American has to do is open their eyes and ears to know that our culture has not improved since 1994. Are our schools any better? Are celebrities any less trashy? Has TV, radio or the media become any less sexually explicit, violent or vulgar? Are our religious institutions any stronger after going through all the scandals? Are salaries improving for average workers? Is the divorce rate improving? Has Aids become any less of a threat? Are there less children living in single parent homes? Just where did those Republicans improve our culture between 1994 and 2006? Despite passing a bunch of laws, the United States government did less during this period than at any time in its history to solve problems for the American people.

The more dependent a society becomes on the law for protecting the rights of its citizens, the greater that society's cultural problems. The law is supposed to serve as the last means of protecting the rights of people. The first means to protect people's rights is their culture. If people don't learn to care for their fellow citizens and respect their rights, all the laws in the world won't change a thing. When politicians claim that changes in the laws will correct the problems, they only blind society to what truly needs to be fixed.

A brave nation always faces up to its problems. The crime problem is a result of numerous social problems, not because penalties for crime are too lenient. If a government official were to say that the solutions to the problems of society could only be solved by society as a whole, or that if people wanted less crime they would have to quit embracing a culture that promoted crime, or that the government by itself can truly do very little without the people joining them in making an effort to change things, then that public servant would become very unpopular and possibly lose their job.

Helvetius, a philosopher of the enlightenment said, "Man is made to be virtuous; and in fact, if force essentially resides in the greater number, and justice consists in the practice of actions useful to the greater number, it is evident that justice is in its own nature always armed with a power sufficient to suppress vice and place men under the necessity of being virtuous."

The problem with Helvetius's statement is that there is no power sufficient to suppress vice and place men under the necessity of being virtuous. Some people will always be involved in vice and a few will even get away with it. Therefore, the most that justice can realistically be expected to accomplish is to contain vice and be an incentive for people to be virtuous. Helvetius failed to understand that virtue is not attained by force. The root of virtue in the virtuous, as well as the root of vice in the criminal, is internal.

Was it the government's lack of power to suppress vice that caused the crime problem? Most criminals don't even know what power the government has, until it's too late. It is always natural for governments to seek more power. This doesn't necessarily mean that our government is evil. It is sometimes a case where those in authority feel that the more power they have, the more they can help. In fairness, if people weren't failing in their responsibilities, the government wouldn't feel compelled to step in and attempt to resolve the problem. The best way for government to help in this situation is to encourage locals to solve the problems of their communities. If a child is learning to walk and then stumbles, do you pick up the child and never let him attempt to walk again? That is what the government has done by not making the focus of the solutions on a local level. It is an abdication of democracy.

Obtaining local control is not so simple. A sense of community must be restored. Democracy and culture require participation. Neither can exist in isolation. The more people participate, the more smoothly democracy functions. If people get involved in their communities, they will negate the justification for the government to become more powerful.

How do we get people to participate? Local institutions could be created to promote participation, and existing institutions could also promote participation. The media could also be used to inform people of the importance of participating in their community.

Schools are also partially responsible for people's lack of participation. Schools usually emphasize the structure of government and society. However, there is usually very little emphasis on the importance and method of participating in both of those structures.

All too often, people hear the word government and they think of some huge, impersonal bureaucracy that has its own interests. Government starts and ends with the people, and there are all types of different levels of government which anyone can get involved in. It is important that people know this so that they are not intimidated.

Perhaps some in power prefer that the government appears unapproachable so that they can continue to decide what's best for people they know nothing about. While it's true that some people are ignorant, it doesn't mean that anyone's participation should be limited. People must be encouraged to become well informed, and participate. America should not have so many people that feel completely disenfranchised from the political process.

What is the person who is going to be committing a homicide next week doing right now? Are they reading the newspaper or watching the news to see what sentences people are getting? Are they going to the library to look at what new statutes the legislature has recently enacted? Of course not. They are probably out on the streets, getting high and looking for action. Who are the only people who can help this person? The people in that person's community. This is a hard and sometimes dangerous task, but people need to reach out to these people. If they don't, it is more than likely they will be exposed to some form of danger from this person anyway.

As long as we are conscious, we have freedom of will. There are times when people undermine their free will by clouding their judgment with drugs and alcohol or other poor decisions. People can then find themselves in situations where they feel compelled to do something wrong, even though they really don't have to. Not knowing how to subdue their bad impulses, they begin to consistently act on them, until someone helps them find their way out of this cycle. This doesn't excuse them for what they've done, but like Dostoevski said, "Nothing is easier than to denounce the evil doer; nothing is more difficult than to understand him."

We can strengthen the good impulses and weaken the bad ones by praising good behavior and rejecting bad behavior in our society. Our media is completely out of control in this regard. We need a more unified front on the part of our institutions on what kind of message we should be sending. Messages promote behavior. Therefore, in order to be united on what messages to send, we have to be united on what behavior to promote.

The problem with American culture today is a result of the various institutions' unwillingness to be united on what norms and values should be promoted. Children are being given mixed messages on how they should behave, yet when they become adults, people are surprised that they don't know how to act. Each institution has a role. When an institution tries to overstep its role in promoting culture, it can undermine other institutions. That institution will then become an overbearing presence, which will ultimately undermine its own capability to influence people. Of all the institutions, the government is the least efficient and least effective to change our culture.

Government is most powerful when it is honest, and when it understands the limitations of its ability to solve problems. It is then that the government can be a catalyst for real change by motivating the individual, the greatest power in a democratic society, to make those choices which will inevitably promote the common good. Government is at its weakest when politicians lie, placing their personal interests above the interests of the people, so that they can pretend to address problems over which they have little control. We need more awareness by those who play a role in the operation of our institutions and they must work in tandem with other institutions if we are to have any culture.

If Republicans still feel that it is more government power that is going to change people's behavior, then they presume to know more than God. God gave man free will, which is both a wonderful and a terrible thing. Yet it was so important to God that we have this free will that He did not intervene when we used it to crucify His only begotten Son. God does not want us to be moral by force, whether it be by His power or that of the government, but by a conscious choice to do the right thing.

Do we need government, good laws and prisons? Surely we do. Yet they will not solve our society's moral quandary. Free will will continue to exist in all its splendor and horror, no matter how much power the government obtains. If we continue to believe that how people choose to apply their free will can be changed by passing a couple of new laws year after year, then like the Romans, our culture will completely collapse under the weight of our dysfunctional civilization.

MULTICULTURALISM

Multiculturalism is the acceptance of living in a society with multiple cultures. There have been numerous societies throughout history that have had multiple cultures, but the failure of the people or leadership to accept that idea has often led to conflicts and even civil wars. While there are a few Americans that resist the idea of multiculturalism, which in its extreme form can lead to hate crimes, most Americans accept that we are a multicultural society.

While culture relies on the unity of institutions, multiculturalism is an acceptance of the divisions of what people believe was, is, and should be. Therefore the question is how do we have any culture in a multicultural society? This is one of the great challenges we face and its resolution is necessary if we are to fix our cultural problem.

While America has established itself as a multicultural society, often called the great melting pot, our political process is opposed to this concept by its very nature. The purpose of politics is to serve the interests of a group. What group you identify yourself with, determines which political party you join to advance your cause. What's at stake is that the winner of the political process is given the opportunity to use the power of the government to promote their belief system.

Both Democrats and Republicans have demonstrated a failure of vision in the manner in which they've addressed governing a multicultural society. Democrats must realize that multiculturalism does not mean going to the extreme of having no culture. It's a fine line to walk between imposing a culture and promoting culture in general. In pursuit of equality, Democrats have refrained from using the government to promote culture. This creates a danger, for as Montesquieu said, "The principle of democracy is corrupted not only when the spirit of equality is extinct, but likewise when they fall into a spirit of extreme equality."

Worrying so much about promoting culture equally, has often paralyzed the liberals' ability to use the government, as well as other institutions, in promoting any culture. True liberalism has been corrupted. To be liberal is to be open-minded. However, some people think that being open-minded requires them to be non-judgmental. This misinterpretation is a simple-minded approach to the multiculturalism dilemma.

If we can recognize negative behavior in our own culture, why not recognize it in other cultures? If we claim to have fundamental values, yet we refuse to apply those values by making judgments on other cultures, we disregard the existence and lose the benefit of having those values. If we value love, then why wouldn't we criticize those who do not act with love, regardless of culture? Intellectual honesty requires a universal application of values.

Being open-minded means not having prejudice to behaviors or ideas, thereby making one capable of evaluating different behaviors or ideas fairly. Being open to debate over a topic does not require one to accept any position that they find ignorant or devious. As a result of political correctness, some groups that promote deviant behavior are not required to be as open to criticism as are the more traditional groups.

It is assumed that traditionalists are not capable of being open-minded since they believe their ways are best. They are ethnocentric and therefore can't fairly criticize any other group. To have values in the first place however, there must be a belief that one way is better than another. Therefore, every group will possess a degree of ethnocentricity. The truly open-minded group does not allow that ethnocentricity to prejudice their evaluation of another group's behavior, or reevaluating their own group's behavior if criticized. The group that refuses to reevaluate their own behavior is not serious about making a multicultural society work.

Without criticism, without debate, how are we to make any changes to improve ourselves? Civilization demands communication. Babies cry because they don't know how to communicate. Adults often wage war because they don't know how to communicate. For communication to be effective, we must be open-minded.

At the same time, it is crucial that we understand what it means to be open-minded. In order to be open-minded, you must have a mind of your own to be open with. By having a mind of your own, and therefore an understanding of yourself and your own culture, you will be capable of understanding others.

Seeing the extreme that Democrats had gone to, Republicans began pushing the envelope towards the other extreme. Republicans began formulating an identity as the party of us versus them, with us being the traditionalists and Christians. This appealed to Americans who were concerned about the moral vacuum created by institutions that weren't promoting any culture. If elected, the Republicans promised to change that by applying traditional Christian values in the way they created, enforced and interpreted the law.

Democrats, who in the past had presented themselves as every man's party, could not offer a united cultural alternative to what Republicans were offering.

Republicans had already seized the high ground by proclaiming to be the party of Christian values. Since the vast majority of Americans identify themselves as Christians, the Democrats were left without any counter moves to offer in the realm of cultural issues that had a chance to be politically effective. What made it all the worse was that Democrats didn't seem to understand their position, or a way to push the debate in a different direction. Only the follies of President George W. Bush could eventually lead Democrats out of the political desert.

Before Bush ruined it, the Republicans' success was largely the result of the hijacking of a radical liberal concept called, "legal realism." Legal realism was the belief that laws are not unchangeable dogmas dictated by God, a king or founding fathers, but rather that laws are political constructs that should be used for positive social change when other institutions aren't up to the task. Legal realism could be used to justify the Civil Rights Act or the Supreme Court's ruling in Roe v. Wade. Republicans adapted this to justify passing tough new laws on criminals, and attempts to stop abortion and gay marriages. The one variation for Republicans is that they didn't see any problem with using God or the founding fathers to justify their cause. Again, it boils down to using the government as a vehicle for social change.

What Republicans have done in recent years can be summed up as preaching to the choir. To convince Christians that we should live in a Christian society does not take a great imagination, nor does it address the reality of our cultural problems. As a Christian it does sound appealing, but we must remember that for religion to have any meaning it must be freely chosen. Even if we were to create a Christian theocracy, which is an extreme that Republicans have not been so foolish to openly propose, how do you force people to be moral?

Regarding the implementation of a Christian society, C.S. Lewis said, "Most of us are not really approaching the subject in order to find out what Christianity says: we are approaching it in the hope of finding support from Christianity for the views of our own party. We are looking for an ally where we are offered either a Master or a Judge."

The Cross is an example of self-sacrifice, not an attempt to seize power. Yet religion does play an important role in our society and must be respected by the other institutions. The Democrats' approach of leaving religious matters to the individual does not take proper account of the fact that religion is perhaps our most important social institution. While the tide is currently in the Democrats' favor, dismissing religion can again have political consequences.

Fixing a multicultural society's cultural problems is not going to happen quickly. This makes it all the more important to identify what will and what won't work. We know that all of our institutions play a role, the question is who is willing to sacrifice for the greater good?

A current disturbing development is that schools across America are gutting arts programs due to a lack of funds. This is despite the fact that children who participate in arts programs and get immersed in some real culture are less likely than other children to get involved in criminal activities. This cut in the arts programs is a threat to the cultures of all Americans. In order to be a multicultural society people must first undergo some cultural development. The arts, throughout history, have played a key role in the ability of people to express and understand their own culture, as well as learn about and respect other cultures. This includes literature, music and the visual arts. As a Christian, listening to Handel's "Messiah", or seeing the work of Michelangelo in the Sistine Chapel, provides another insight to understanding my religion.

The demise of art reflecting the demise of culture is not a new phenomenon. Art and culture have always gone hand in hand. Diderot's critique of a pastorale by Boucher in 1765 is a humorous demonstration of just how subtle the decadence in the arts were at that time:

"What colors, what variety, what wealth of objects and ideas! The man has everything except truth. Where has anybody seen shepherds so elegantly dressed? What occasion has brought together in open country, under a bridge, far from any house, women, men, children, cows, sheep, dogs, bunches of straw, fire and water, pots and pans? What is that well dressed, voluptuous woman doing? Are those children hers? And this man carrying fire that he's about to heap on her head, is he the husband? What a clutter of disparates! It's obviously absurd. But one can't look away from it. One lusts after it, the extravagance is inimitable. It is magic."

A multicultural society must have a multiplicity of real cultures. We're not talking about a difference of opinion, but rather a difference in the way people choose to live their lives. While humans have never been very good at compromise, thus the difficulty in creating a multicultural society, different cultures have much more in common today than ever before. At the root of the various cultural approaches to living, people are just seeking a concept that will make their lives easier. Therefore, despite all the rhetoric, most people like driving cars, using phones and computers, eating in restaurants, using a shower and so on ... Today, the only group that truly sets themselves apart from the rest, is the Amish. If we are eventually destroyed by global warming, they will have been the only ones that were right. Yet, you never hear them making much of a fuss. Maybe they should.

While people claim to embrace multiculturalism, today we see a lot less of any culture being promoted to our youth. Sometimes, having a group of people from different ethnicities will not even result in cultural diversity. I've known young whites, latinos, and blacks who are all similarly culturally oriented. They listen to the same music, play the same video games, talk the same, have the same core beliefs, watch the same TV shows and engage in the same behaviors. They share the commercial American culture. Some people might think this cross ethnic commercial culture might be the answer, but there is one caveat. I'm talking about gang bangers in our prison system.

The American commercial culture is empty. It has no spirit. It cannot replace our traditional cultures that have developed over centuries and have the depth to give individuals a solid identity. Without this identity, our youth are rudderless in the sea of temptation that our society has become. Real American culture, as opposed to the ever changing commercial variety, is a synthesis of all the cultures that came together to make America a great multicultural society. That's what we need to promote.

THE LEGAL POLITICAL SYSTEM

In the ultimate power game, judges and prosecutors have failed to defend the legal system in the endless tug of war between politics and justice. Through the use of populist rhetoric, which is what politicians like Hitler and Mussolini used to take democratic states and warp them into their own beastly images, contemporary politicians have subtly stripped the legal system of its objective of serving justice. Despite politics and justice being incompatible, serving political agendas has been made the new objective of our legal system. Rather than recognizing their professional obligation to keep justice and politics separated, many judges and prosecutors goose-step right along with politicians, since they too are elected and have political aspirations. Vengeance is not justice, yet the language of tough on crime rhetoric is completely vengeance oriented. Whereas a legal justice system is run by judges and prosecutors of an objective nature, the legal political system is run by demagogues.

A demagogue is someone who gains power and popularity by arousing the emotions and prejudices of people. In just about every election, you see these divisive, ad hominem arguments being used to bolster the candidates' image. It's a lot easier to frame a political campaign against an unpopular issue than it is to run against an opponent. Elections have become advertising campaigns where the winner is whichever candidate has the most money to spend on selling themselves as tough on crime, against gay marriage, for less taxes, and for or against whatever else is popular at the time. Karl Rove has made a name for himself doing this nationally for George W. Bush and other Republicans.

The problem with winning at any cost is that it undermines the very principles that America is based on. We are called the United States for a reason; unity is a core value in our democracy. This doesn't mean we can't have dissent, but rather that as Americans we are all part of a brotherhood or fraternity. Without that belief, equality is just something we pay lip service to. When politicians falsely frame every issue as us versus them, they slowly destroy the fabric that holds America together. Yet if you ask them, they'll tell you they're very patriotic.

The irony is that these very people who wrap themselves in the flag the most, value the concept of what America is, the least. They're willing to polarize a nation to serve their own political interests, while we live in a time when it's crucial we work together to solve some big problems. When people say they love America, what they really mean is that they love themselves, and their fellow Americans like them. Loving America though means loving it all, the bad and the good. The pretty with the ugly, the mountains and the mole hills.

What America is really about is taking things to the next level. We will not be enslaved by our past, no obstacle will stand in our way. From the arts to the sciences, we're going to make things better. We will never be satisfied. Every generation must not only pass the torch, but raise the bar. That's the real America and all Americans are called to share in that responsibility. Is that what today's politicians are offering? A real American politician named John Quincy Adams warned us, "Remember Democracy never lasts long. It soon wastes, exhausts, murders itself. There never was a democracy yet that did not commit suicide. It is vain to say that democracy is less vain, less proud, less selfish, less ambitious, or less avaricious than aristocracy or monarchy. It is not true, in fact, and nowhere appears in history. Those passions are the same in all men, under all forms of simple government, and when unchecked, produce the same effect of fraud, violence, and cruelty."

A democracy without a justice system, is no democracy. The legal political system put in its place, is the first step towards a democracy murdering itself and becoming a police state. Criminals harm others for personal gain. When politicians, judges, and prosecutors punish people for personal political gain, they succumb to the same devious mental plane as the criminal, when the criminal was rationalizing the commission of their crimes.

The media has not been very critical of how politicians use crime to gain public favor. This is because the media also uses crime to sell their product and, just about every day, the television news or newspapers have crime as their lead story. This has made it easy for politicians to appeal to the emotions and prejudices of their constituents who are bombarded with crime stories daily by the media. Then add the fact that every night, during prime time, there are television shows with crime central to the plot: C.S.I., Cops, America's Most Wanted, Boston Legal, Cold Case, etc...

Considering that it is what society watches every day, it is no mystery why every politician wants to be viewed as tough on crime. The problem is that in their zeal to appear tough, politicians have implemented many policies that our states will simply be unable to afford. These policies were based on best case scenario assumptions on how the economy would perform. I've never heard a politician talk about how much money any of these new laws will cost. Maybe they can't, because then they'd be labeled soft on crime. After all, reality shouldn't interfere with politics.

The economics of this will be a weight that eventually pushes many states to adopt reforms. The fact that some states will fall into a fiscal crisis before these reforms are made, shows just how little foresight politicians have. We live in a society without depth. Most issues are covered in a thirty-second sound bite. Our politicians and media have no problem avoiding tackling complex issues. The ratings dictate our national dialogue.

Nobody batted an eyelash when the 1996 Antiterrorism and Effective Death Penalty Act, passed in response to the Oklahoma City bombing, allowed our government to set time limits that kept prisoners from being able to file appeals in Federal Court. Throwing people's lives away on technicalities is a reflection of a politicized legal system that focuses more on the imagery of toughness than the principle of justice. In free nations, the condemned should always have the opportunity to appeal decisions when the appeal has merit. If a prisoner files an appeal with merit, it would be the most cowardly of governments that would ignore those facts or arguments that call into question the validity of a conviction simply because a time limit has passed. Is not a tyrant an authority who goes to an extreme simply to avoid acknowledging wrongful actions or mistakes?

Is a law degree something you get out of a cracker jack box in the United States? If not, how can prisoners be expected to know more law than the attorneys who represented them? That's what they'll have to do to be able to figure out where their attorney made mistakes. Prisoners don't get a free trip to law school, they have to teach themselves the law in the prison library. Most of them haven't even graduated from high school! Only the smarter inmates who can figure out where the government violated their rights, in a timely fashion, have a chance to get a shot at real justice? Regardless of innocence? This sounds like an experiment you do with rats in a maze. Only if they figure it out in a certain time do they get the cheese.

A police state must, at every chance possible, chip away at due process rights to maintain efficiency while accumulating mass and power. Politicians need to quit using tragedies to justify seizing more power for the State. When laws are created as a result of an emotional response to a tragedy, our politicians' credibility is undermined. Only insecure politicians would demonstrate a complete lack of confidence in democracy by passing new laws to restore the voters' faith in government. At times, it is necessary to pass new laws. However, those laws should serve to promote the common good, not the popularity and re-election of a professional politician.

John F. Kennedy said politicians should, "have faith in their ultimate sense of justice, faith in their ability to honor courage and respect judgment, and faith that in the long run they will act unselfishly for the good of the nation. It is that kind of faith on which democracy is based, not simply the often frustrated hope that public opinion will at all times under all circumstances promptly identify itself with the public interest."

Politicians must be ready to do things that might not help in their next election. Is that too much to ask when our soldiers are risking their lives every day? Politicians have to realize that their responsibility is to use their authority to attain the goals that our government was established for. Those goals are dictated by the Preamble to the United States Constitution.

"We, the people of the United States, in order to form a more perfect union, establish justice, insure domestic tranquility, provide for the common defense, promote the general welfare, and secure the blessings of liberty to ourselves and our posterity, do ordain and establish this Constitution of the United States of America."

That little opening salvo to our Constitution summarizes the entire philosophy of why we have a government. Any debate about what's constitutional can be referred to the preamble. If the government fails to strive for those goals mentioned in the preamble, it loses its justification to exist. It is the responsibility of those in authority to make sure that their decisions are consistent with those goals.

The Founding Fathers risked their lives to create this nation. Today's politicians are far more calculating. Before committing to a position, they often feel they have to consult the polls. True leadership is not about winning a popularity contest, however. I understand the dilemma politicians in a democracy face. They can only stay in power as long as they are popular, but doing what's best is not always popular. In that situation, John Quincy Adams said, "Highly as I reverenced the authority of my constituents, and bitter as would have been the cup of resistance to their declared will … I would have defended their interest against their inclinations and incurred every possible additions to their resentment, to save them from the vassalage of their own delusions."

Vassalage is right. What do you think believing that you're dependent on the government to solve all your problems means? Freedom means accepting responsibility for the state of our society. It means the people acting together to achieve a common goal. It does not mean allowing charlatan politicians to politicize our legal system so they can pretend to solve problems. The people have to choose between a legal political and legal justice system. Unlike the politicians, I want people to know that they do in fact have a choice.

WHO WATCHES OVER GOVERNMENT

One basic tenant of democracy is that power must be shared. This is the underlying principle that the French philosopher Montesquieu used to develop the Separation of Powers Doctrine, which America's founding fathers applied when they created our three branches of government. In Montesquieu's time, the 18th century, European society was divided by class. Montesquieu was not interested in eliminating conflict between classes, since he considered class rivalry a sign of health in a democracy. Instead, he envisioned a system where by sharing power, the classes would have the opportunity to advance their interests in a civilized forum, while at the same time checking each other's extremes so as to advance the common good.

Comprehending Montesquieu's logic in contriving the Separation of Powers Doctrine is facilitated by knowing his first book, *Persian Letters*. In that classic appears the tale of the Troglodytes. The Troglodytes were a people who chose to be completely governed by their self-interest, thus their motto, "I will live happy." Without any concern for the common good, the Troglodytes' self-centered agenda led to families being destroyed, their economy ruined, property lost, and the population ultimately decimated by a plague. The main theme of the story is that virtue and liberty are inseparable. If the government ceases to be virtuous, freedom will disappear. This thinking is a prelude to the Separation of Powers Doctrine in that the purpose of the checks and balances is to maintain public virtue.

Montesquieu's book, *Spirit of Laws* argues that there is only one way to preserve liberty, and that is by having a government where "power stops power." In a warning against monopolizing the three branches, he states that liberty is lost when, "the same man, or the same body of princes, or of nobles, or of people exercise these three powers." Montesquieu also claimed that even if one clique held both the executive and legislative branches, that it would suffocate liberty.

Clearly in our day, power is not shared by the classes as both Republicans and Democrats have sold out the poor to pander to the interests of corporate America, the upper class. This has been the case in just about every piece of legislation passed from 2001 through 2006. The irony is how politicians spin their legislation, sometimes termed corporate welfare, as being pro-business. The propaganda is that unless politicians cater to the insurance, oil, credit industries, etc..., as though they are mystical gods who must be paid the appropriate homage, the economy won't be able to function. Big business has taken Ayn Rand's economic philosophy from *Atlas Shrugged* and applied it politically to extort laws that are in their favor. "Play by my rules or I'll take my ball and go to China," would be the appropriate motto of big business in America today, and its so-called pro-business politicians who have made that possible. If anyone wants to know exactly how working conditions would be without government regulation, please read Upton Sinclair's *The Jungle*, which depicts the horrors of meat packing in Chicago in the early twentieth century. Or, look at any of the sweatshops run by American corporations in the Third World.

Americans need to understand how dangerous it is to put all their eggs in one basket and let one political party run the country. During the Bill Clinton years, we saw that with a Republican Congress and a Democratic president, our government operated much more efficiently than it did under the all Republican reign from 2001 through 2006. Although Bush and his fellow Republicans espouse the virtue of fiscal conservatism, they simply could not restrain themselves from the prospect of having it all. Whatever the rhetoric on balanced budgets was in the past, their human nature trumped their ideology. This will be a costly lesson for Americans to learn as government spending has skyrocketed, while tax cuts by the same leadership have reduced federal revenue by billions of dollars. The result is massive deficits that must eventually be paid back with interest. Of course it's not those responsible for this mismanagement who will suffer, but rather the poor, who are more dependent on an efficient government, because they rely to a greater degree on its services.

We are now facing problems in both the credit card and mortgage industry. The mortgage industry gets more publicity for its problems, because the result is people losing their homes to foreclosure. Now, all of a sudden, we hear our politicians are trying to address these issues through new legislation, such as freezing interest rates. Where have they been?

Are we to believe that the government is unaware of what goes on in each of these multi-billion dollar industries? Where's the oversight? We don't regulate how money is loaned? The loan shark is one of the cornerstones of organized crime, yet there's no rules governing interest by our credit card and mortgage industries? Rather than point out to the public how they failed to enforce existing laws to prevent this crisis from occurring, politicians claim we need more laws. Since both political parties are dirty with the money they've been given to look the other way, they are not going to "check" each other and acknowledge their combined failure to oversee these industries.

As if big business had not profited enough during Bush's tenure, Bush had the audacity to nominate corporate lawyer Harriet Miers to the Supreme Court. Many criticisms were made about this nominee, and neither party was very pleased with her. The attacks generally fell along party lines and missed the point of why Supreme Court nominees should not be selected on a political basis. John Roberts, a conservative, was eventually confirmed to become the new Chief Justice of the Supreme Court.

Everyone loses when politicians choose to politicize our legal system. Most Americans support their politicians in nominating judges that have their political views, without realizing that by doing so, they are eliminating the power of the judicial branch to act as a check against either of the other branches. The tree of democracy is dependent on the vitality of its branches.

It is imperative that when making choices for Supreme Court and Federal Court judges, the process must favor apolitical candidates. A politically minded judge has a conflict of loyalty between the Constitution and the group whose political orientation he or she advocates. While everyone likes the idea of a judge being on his or her side, fairness requires that judges be on nobody's side, but on that of the Constitution.

One of the reasons we don't elect people to the Supreme Court is that they have a role in protecting the rights of minorities, which is not always a popular thing to do. To keep America from a tyranny of the majority, we will need our presidents to nominate objective people to the Supreme Court. Both parties need to play a role in promoting a healthy judiciary and depoliticizing the process of nominating judges.

Term limits appear to be the only institutional check on power currently functioning. Without them, we would one day have to tell George W. Bush something along the lines of what Fénelon told King Louis XIV:

"Sire: For forty years your ministers have violated all the ancient laws of the state so as to enhance your power. They have increased your revenue and your expenditures to the infinite and impoverished all of France for the sake of your luxury at court. They have made your name odious.

For twenty years they have made the French nation intolerable to its neighbors by bloody wars. We have no allies because we only wanted slaves. Meanwhile, your people are starving. Sedition is spreading and you are reduced to either letting it spread unpunished or resorting to massacring the people that you have driven to desperation."

Today, you can't get around the fact that voters have the ultimate responsibility of putting good, intelligent people into positions of power. If the people elect losers, they will have to suffer the consequences of giving power to people incapable of serving the nation's best interests. If the voters elect partisan politicians whose concern for the public interest is not as important as serving their self-interest, then one must expect them to select partisan judges with the same agendas. The Separation of Powers is a good doctrine, but it cannot be a substitute for the voters in watching over their government.

RELIGION, POLITICS &
JUSTICE

After the re-election of George W. Bush, there was a lot of bragging by conservatives that the strategy of using topics like gay marriage to appeal to religious voters was what won them the election. They went so far as to claim that Bush's victory was a victory for moral values! Is this really a case of amazing grace, or the usual political path of amazing graft?

An election funded by millions of dollars in corporate money, that will be paid back through the passing of legislation that will favor those corporations over the interests of the common voter, being viewed as a victory for moral values, is an obscene proposition. One is forced to question whether these people who bring religion into politics really care about God at all.

During the 2004 presidential campaign, it was very disappointing to see people in both parties presenting their candidates as though they were the second coming of the Messiah. Bush didn't help matters much with his second inauguration speech where he talked about saving the world from tyranny. What's clear is that the egos in American politics today are huge.

I understand the appeal of having one's religious values institutionalized by the government. As a Catholic, it seems a perfectly natural responsibility for an institution to fill, as the Church plays a large role in maintaining the value system that we have, and passing it on from generation to generation.

It is not surprising that this ideology also appeals to some Protestants. Some Protestant churches are similar to Catholicism in their firm structure and adherence to tradition. It was King Henry VIII who proposed a middle way, "via media," which is to say Catholicism without a Pope, while creating the Church of England (referred to as Episcopal Church, in America). Henry VIII had no problem mixing religion and politics. Whereas he focused on nationalizing religion, creating the Anglican Church, conservatives today work in the opposite direction to establish religious dominance over the government.

What is surprising is that those less structured Protestant faiths, some of which go so far as to abhor the idea of "institutionalized" religion, feel that the U.S. government is the institution they should now use to in fact institutionalize their religion. However, it is human nature to try and organize things according to one's beliefs and make sure that it lasts, so it can be passed down to one's children and the following generations. Everyone, despite what they claim, would like to have their views and beliefs win, take the day, dominate, be adhered to, or however you want to put it. The one way to do this is by having the government pass a law and thereby enshrine or institutionalize the beliefs of your party or faith. This is what makes those politicians who claim they'll advocate faith, so appealing.

Even if we don't expect a politician to get any laws changed, we hope that the people we elect have a sense of morality. People want to believe that when a person says they follow the moral guidance of a religion that they will be a righteous leader. Throughout history however, many political leaders have claimed to be followers of a religion, but I don't remember any that have been able to follow the example of their religion perfectly. King David would be one example amongst many. Read 2 Samuel 11:1-27 for more on that. Are we to understand that George W. Bush is closer to God than King David?

The problems these claims of righteousness create is that when people build up their political candidacy on the issue of their being a Christian, and then they turn around and do something which could be perceived as unchristian, they can undermine the credibility of a religion. "You who boast of the law, do you dishonor God by breaking the law? For as it is written, 'Because of you the name of God is reviled among the Gentiles.'" Romans 2:23-24.

Let's examine how both Moses and St. Paul would be treated if they'd lived in Texas during the time that George W. Bush was Governor. One day, Moses is walking down the street minding his own business. He then sees a cop beating up on someone who had tried to flee. This is a familiar sight for those who watch the television show, "Cops". So, old Moses doesn't like what he sees and decides to intervene. Moses snatches up the cop, kills him, and hides the body in the sand, just like he did to the Egyptian who struck a Hebrew in Exodus 2:11-12. In those days an Egyptian was the law, and a Hebrew had no rights, like a criminal. If Moses had been arrested for that in Texas, he would have never had the opportunity to go up on Mount Sinai to get those Ten Commandments, which many people would like to post in courthouses all over the country. The same courthouses that would, more often than not, kill poor Moses. Certainly with George W. Bush as Governor, Moses would not have gotten a stay of execution.

As far as St. Paul is concerned, if he'd done what he did to St. Stephen in Texas, Bush might have gone down to death row to do the lethal injection himself. You see, before St. Paul became a Christian, he was named Saul and was banging for a rough crew known as the Hebrews. In Acts 7:58 and 8:1-3, it is clear that St. Paul persecuted Christians, including stoning St. Stephan to death. Under Bush's reign, St. Paul might have been executed before he had the opportunity to write the large portion of the New Testament that he is credited for, some of which Bush has probably used quotes from.

To be fair, Bush is not the only person that claims the Bible justifies the death penalty. Under the laws of Leviticus, anyone that curses their mother and father, homosexuals, fortune tellers, adulterers, and many others, should be put to death. If we practice the laws of Leviticus, we could solve our social security problem very quickly. However, those rules were intended for the righteous to carry out. Since there aren't any completely righteous people though, God felt we needed a new way to look at how we deal with sinners. There was nothing wrong with the original law, but there was something wrong with man. That is one of the reasons God gave us the New Testament. "Let the one among you who is without sin be the first to throw a stone at her." John 8:7.

Those who quote, "an eye for an eye, a tooth for a tooth," Matthew 5:8, don't understand the totality of the Mosaic law. If they did, they'd know that under that law, they too would have to be put to death. Matthew 5:28, defines the fullness of what the law, "You shall not commit adultery," means. "But I say to you, everyone who looks at a woman with lust has already committed adultery in his heart."

Christians are supposed to recognize that they are sinners who have broken the old covenant, Mosaic law, and need Christ to save them from the consequences of their behavior. That is why He is called the Savior. Christians must therefore be very careful in how they judge people. "For as you judge, so will you be judged, and the measure with which you measure will be measured to you." Matthew 7:2. For a Christian to punish someone under the full measure of the Mosaic law, would be a rejection of the new Covenant that Christ died to establish. When looked at from that perspective, no true Christian can be for the death penalty. This doesn't diminish its popularity, and I would not expect a great popular moralist like Bush to be the one to abandon this practice.

A leader is forced to make many decisions which impact the lives of many people. Those decisions can range from cuts in spending, which might cost people their jobs or medical care, to going to war, which will cost people their lives. While those decisions might be completely necessary, they could also be inconsistent with the teachings of Christianity. If the government would have literally followed Christ's teaching to turn the other cheek, then it would not have considered using military force to respond to the attacks on Fort Sumter, The Maine, The Lusitania, Pearl Harbor, and the World Trade Center. Yet, that would defeat the main purpose of having a government.

The purpose of government is to help keep our society safe and organized. This has many benefits in that it allows us to go on about our lives with a degree of confidence that if we do the right things, get educated, work, and don't break laws, we can have a good life. However, let someone attempt to disturb that order and we expect our government to take care of business, with bullets, bombs, and missiles. We don't want our government to run to our enemies with a Bible in hand and attempt to proselytize the Gospel.

This doesn't mean that we can't have religious people in government. It should be recognized though that the role of being a government official is a worldly one, whereas the following of a religion generally calls people to set aside the world and pursue the divine. The beginning of having a government in the Old Testament shows how incompatible religion and government are the moment you step away from being a theocracy, "Samuel was displeased when they asked for a king to judge them. He prayed to the Lord, however, who said in answer: 'Grant the people's every request. It is not you they reject, they are rejecting Me as their King.'" Samuel 8:6-7.

For those who claim to believe in the Bible, this story of Samuel is one of the most important and overlooked passages in the history of mankind. From the point where God says they are rejecting Him, by choosing a leader for themselves, every government that has claimed to be run by God, a theocracy, has been a counterfeit. Up until that point in Samuel, the Jewish people had the only true theocracy in human history. Once they made that break with God and rejected Him as their leader, every political leader in human history that claimed they governed by God's will was a fraud. Those leaders either hadn't read Samuel, and were ignorant of the history of the Bible, or they knew the history but realized the masses didn't. The result is that time and time again political leaders have tried to cloak themselves and their political agendas with religion in an attempt to justify themselves and their agendas.

This does not mean that there is no place for God in our body politic. What we should hope for from those who have faith and get into politics is that they act with as much mercy and compassion as possible, while performing the sometimes brutal duties which government office entails. Having authority over millions of people is an awesome responsibility and pursuing the noble ideal of following God while dealing with worldly affairs is a difficult high wire to walk. It is by actions, not empty rhetoric, that we will be able to identify the faithful both in politics and everyday life.

Knowing the challenges we must face in our attempts to follow a religion, those who strive for leadership positions must realize that the more they wear religion on their sleeve to get votes, the more people they will inevitably turn away from religion, once they get into the dirty business of worldly leadership. This is not to say that a person should deny or hide their beliefs, but rather they should understand the implications of their beliefs and be humble in how they approach God.

"When you pray, do not be like the hypocrites who love to pray in the synagogues and on the street corners so that others may see them. Amen, I say to you, they have received their reward. But when you pray go to your inner room, close the door, and pray to your Father in secret. And your father who sees in secret will repay you." Matthew 6:5-6.

We are all called to have a personal relationship with God. It is through that personal relationship that we can derive the benefits of our religious beliefs. When we choose to have that relationship, it is not to be shown off to impress people, or for politicians to get votes. It is a very serious matter, and our founding fathers correctly understood that it wasn't for the government to establish that relationship. Religion is in fact so precious that it is degraded when the government tries to meddle with it.

What does the Bible say about imposing Christianity? "Then Jesus approached and said to them, 'All power in heaven and on earth has been given to me. Go, therefore, and make disciples of all nations, baptizing them in the name of the Father, and of the Son and of the Holy Spirit, teaching them to observe all that I have commanded you. And behold, I am with you always, until the end of the age.'" Matthew 28:18-20.

This beautiful closing to the Gospel of Matthew is not just pretty words to real Christians. They mean that Christ is all powerful and can make anything happen. However, rather than impose His will, which is what He will do at the Last Judgment, He gives us the opportunity to go out and "teach" others to observe what He has commanded them. Nowhere does He state that it's the government's job to impose the belief. Christ does not want to change governments but rather people. He knows that to change a person you must teach them, rather than impose a law upon them. He wants people to do right by choice, not by threat of a legal sanction. This is the entire message of the New Testament.

If one were to believe that man is saved by law, then there would be no difference between the New Testament, the Old Testament and the Koran. The Old testament and the Koran preach that man is saved by following the law. The New Testament teaches that while the law is valid, man is not. Therefore man can only be saved by Christ. Any Christian who claims that salvation comes through passing any kind of law is an apostate, not only for preaching a false doctrine of salvation, but because they are rejecting the obligation of the Christian to "teach".

Of course, it's much easier to simply pass a law than it is to go out and talk to people we don't really like, and teach them about the greatness of God's love through Jesus Christ. There will be times when it is appropriate for political leaders to make references to God. Those times will be few and far between, as God's name was not meant to be carelessly thrown around and used in vain.

Religion is a double-edged sword. In the right hands it can unite people and encourage them to perform great deeds. In the wrong hands, it can cause division, backbiting and doubt. While performing their governmental duties on behalf of all the people, regardless of their differences in belief, it would be best for politicians to keep that sword in its scabbard.

LEVIATHAN

The English philosopher Thomas Hobbes believed that man, in his natural state, would constantly be at war with his fellow man. Hobbes said, "the life of man would be solitary, poor, nasty, brutish and short." This was his rationale behind the construction of Leviathan. Leviathan was the metaphor Hobbes used to describe the artificial body that is the state. Its sometimes beastly demeanor was justified by its role in keeping the peace. Hobbes felt that since keeping the peace was the primary responsibility of the state, that all power should be granted to the state to obtain that goal, and whatever rights the people might have should take a back seat to that authority. What good is a right without security?

In recent years, the American people have been conditioned to support this view of government. To fight crime and now terrorism, Americans are allowing the government to become a Leviathan. This is what is offered as a trade-off to securing whatever rights remain after the government is given more power. Every time a bill is passed in the name of fighting crime or terrorism, Americans lose just a little bit more of their democracy. America becomes the leader in the world in locking people up, and who is protesting? A functioning democracy should not have this crime problem. Yet, people accept this policy as necessary for the same reason most Americans accepted that the war in Iraq was necessary, because the authorities told them so. Since those in power feel that it is thanks to the government that we have our freedoms, not our founding fathers or even those who actually do the work to make America what it is, they have no fear that anyone would dare question them when they say that the power lies in their hands to make everything right. Certainly an educated electorate who understood what democracy was made of, would have misgivings about any authority making such claims. Not in America however. There was only one person, Senator Feingold, who spoke out against the flaws in the Patriot Act!

The problem that inevitably arises is when we find out that our Leviathan is more talk than substance. This was one of the main points in my novel Preemptive Strike. Why should the character Paul submit to the rules of the state when the state is incapable of protecting him or his daughter from becoming victims of the Russian Mafia? Should he not be allowed to take certain liberties to secure his rights? Most states would say no. They'd like to be the hero, the savior, and the solution.

Every election season brings the promise by politicians that they will keep the people safe. This message is very popular despite the fact that these politicians have failed miserably. We won't focus on 9/11, which occurred only five years after the 1996 Antiterrorism and Effective Death Penalty Act was passed, or the incompetent response by government to hurricane Katrina, after billions were spent creating a Department of Homeland Security that was supposed to coordinate government agencies so that they would work together better during a disaster. Instead of these easy pickings, I will focus on crime, where many are convinced Leviathan has had some success, by being a beast on criminals.

The numbers aren't as impressive as our government would have people believe. Leviathan has its own propaganda machine and far too many people are benefiting from the current policy to bother and question the conventional wisdom. To put things in perspective, let me use a football analogy. Let's say the Green Bay Packers put up 50 points on the Chicago Bears in a beat down. Then, the next game they play against each other, the Packers win but score twenty percent less points. Would the sports columnists in Chicago hail the defense as improving since this time they only gave up 40 points? If a sports columnist dared utter such a foolish claim, Bears fans would hang him in effigy, or think he had a sick sense of humor. Yet, when it comes to murders in our nation's cities where the numbers are often much greater than 50 and represent something far more significant than points in a football game, politicians applaud themselves when the numbers go down from say 115 to 100 in a city like Milwaukee, Wisconsin or from 550 to 475 in a city like Chicago. Should Leviathan be allowed to boast about these numbers? When the murder rates go back up, shall we cut down on Leviathan's consumption? We feed Leviathan with much money and power and should expect a reasonable return on the investment. Does the average American feel safe after dark in any large inner city? Hold on! After billions spent and millions incarcerated we aren't safe? Is it not true that anyone can be struck by crime anywhere; at work, at school, at home? Is Leviathan really protecting us?

Often times, you'll hear Leviathan boasting about the need for all this power so that it can "deter" crime, and therefore we should accept the passage of any law it deems beneficial. Is this the most efficient method of deterring people from becoming criminals? Take someone who is considering becoming a drug dealer as an example. Should he be deterred by the fact that Leviathan will lock him up in an institution where he'll get three meals a day and a warm bed, or that a dope fiend or rival drug dealer might kill him for his drugs and money? Should the drunk considering driving drunk be more concerned with a couple of months in jail or life in a wheelchair or even death as a result of a crash?

In an educated society, there are many deterrents that require very little expense or power handed over to Leviathan. Yet, you'll never hear Leviathan's ministers, like a judge, tell the drug dealer to stop dealing drugs because he might get murdered. That wouldn't be politically profitable. Hobbes had it right that if you believe the state should be the one to rely on for protection, that it is indeed a beast, and beasts tend to be very hungry and self-serving.

Hobbes rationalization for a Leviathan type of government was based on his view that man was by nature a savage. The problem is that this eliminated the possibility of culture and human development. If we empower the government to be brutal because we believe we are nothing but savages, then that is where our destiny lies.

Right now, we have over two million people in prison in America. Ninety percent of these prisoners will get out one day and two-thirds of those will be coming back to prison shortly thereafter. That's 1.2 million crimes we have to look forward to by our current inmate population, on top of the millions of felons already released from prisons, plus all the future first time offenders. The increasing harshness of Leviathan in recent years in its treatment of the prison population, by giving lengthier prison sentences and making prisons harsher by granting prison authorities more power to punish inmates as well as reducing the number of privileges, will result in a much tougher and more violent group coming out of America's prisons in the coming years. Score one for Leviathan since even when it fails, it can do no wrong. Rising crime rates will simply mean Leviathan needs more money, more cops, more prisons and most importantly more new laws.

In Preemptive Strike, I show the dark side of prostitution and what sort of shady characters that sort of enterprise supports, in an attempt to persuade people not to solicit prostitutes. The message of art should be that we are called to higher things than simply following the desires of our natural state, whatever that might be. We are a special creature endowed with the capacity for introspection. Preemptive Strike closes with the attorney Misha declaring that, "The answer has never lied in the creation of new laws, but rather in the development of the character of humanity." We shortchange ourselves when we accept the illusion that Leviathan will solve all our problems. Do we need a government? Of course we do, but there has to be a balance. The more we develop as a society, the less problems we'll need the government to solve. The question therefore is not how to empower the state but how to use the state to encourage the development of society.

Threats will always pop up, and when they do, Leviathan will lick its chops. The world can be a frightening place, but anyone that tells you they can make it anything else is a liar and disciple of Leviathan. Leviathan will die only when people choose not to live in fear and believe themselves worthy of a higher form of government.

CREDIT OVERDUE

Politicians, which includes judges and district attorneys since they are elected and take part in a political process, have made great efforts in recent years in being credited as tough on crime. It usually didn't take much effort, just being for the latest fad in new tough laws. None of these people actually went out on the streets and chased down rapists and robbers. Yet this did not not stop them from becoming legends in their own minds, and even in the minds of many of their constituents.

As I appraise the attitudes of leaders in the way they address crime, as well as how people in our society expect politicians to address crime, I notice a resemblance to the comic book heroes that have become such a popular element in American culture. Have we been conditioned to accept this role playing? The predominant theme of these comics is that the good super-hero triumphs over the evil villains. In real life, we have no shortage of real villains committing crimes in every corner of our country. Where are Batman, Spiderman or even Superman when you need them? That's where our politicians step in to fill the vacuum. They will be our super-heroes they assure us, at least that's what they imply when they tell us how tough on crime they are, or will be.

When elections come around, the best way for politicians to attack their opponents is to question their tough on crime bona fides. If their opponent shows any hesitation to put on the cape of tough on crime rhetoric, they will be denigrated for being soft on crime. Running for political office is now as much about being able to present the image of a super-hero as anything else. Who can we trust to swoop down and pass another law to save us?

As the crime rate dropped in the 1990's, our super-hero politicians were quick to take credit, and this lasted pretty much until the summer of 2005 in Milwaukee, Wisconsin. At that point people started realizing that a return to higher crime rates was occurring. Immediately, our super-hero politicians went into hiding. Politicians and their supporters began casting blame on the people living in crime ridden communities for the increased violence. On TV and on the radio, they said things like, "They need to take responsibility for their community," or "It all starts in the home."

Many of these people who now felt that the community should solve its own problems were not saying that in the past elections. Isn't it a little disingenuous for all these tough on crime super-heroes to tell us the solution begins in the community after they've said for years that they were going to deter crime with tougher laws and fatter prison sentences? After getting laws passed, more than doubling the prison population, and spending hundreds of millions of dollars in tax revenue that was taken from schools and other public services which actually helped the people in crime ridden communities, now we hear that it's up to "those" people to solve their problems for themselves. Don't be outraged though, there is always a heavy price to pay for societies that place their faith in false saviors.

Now the truth begins to trickle out. When the homicide rates go up and false credit can no longer be taken, it is finally acknowledged that no matter how many prisons we build, laws are passed, or cops are added, the government can never take away the one equation that determines whether people commit crimes, free will.

The government cannot save a society from itself, nor can it impose culture. What you are seeing with this crime surge is just the tip of the iceberg. During the 1990's, many states like Wisconsin could afford to live in a fantasy world since the economy was doing fairly well. During times like that, rhetoric begins to count more than actual deeds since the good times mask all. Now we are stuck with a huge prison system that is a hungry parasite sucking away money from schools, health care, road construction, parks, and everything else we need government for. Nothing has really been planned for the long term. Instead of a plan we've got a lot of hot air about being tough from a bunch of self-serving politicians. How much longer can this go on?

Crime is a very serious problem in Milwaukee, and a couple of other counties in Wisconsin. When representatives from other counties that have had maybe one homicide in the last five years come into the debate, screaming about how "we" need to be tough on crime, and add the death penalty and more prisons, those representatives who actually have to deal with the crime problem need to tell those other politicians that the problem of their constituents are not to be used for their personal political gain. Crime is a catchy political issue, but every time crime rates rise, politicians from low crime districts so vocal about the issue have sacrificed nothing by pretending to address the problem. They will then flip from the language of "we" to the language of "they" in a heart beat.

As the murders continued, Mayor Tom Barrett attempted to come up with some ways to address the crime problem in Milwaukee. He immediately came under heavy criticism, despite the fact that it wasn't he who had claimed that passing things like "truth in sentencing" or "three strikes", would deter crime. He had never claimed to be a super-hero politician. Now, with all the money gone, Tom Barrett is left to scramble to find money simply to pay for police overtime to monitor high crime areas.

The judges are another case in point. How can they sit on the bench for decades looking the victims of crime, or their families, in the eye and telling them that the sentences they are handing out on criminals will deter crime. If that was true, the incident that led them to be in court would have never occurred due to the past sentences where these judges made this same claim. Is there a magical number of times that judges need to make this claim, for it to come true? Doubtful, but the honorable frauds proceed as if that were the case.

Victims need to demand more. On an emotional level, it's satisfying to know that the bad guy will be going to prison. However, don't think this judge or prosecutor invented the idea of punishment. While they often act like they are doing the victims of crime a big favor, rest assured that criminals were getting punished long before they ever made their way into the courthouse. Victims of crime need to realize that despite all the self-serving rhetoric in the courthouse, the problem of crime has come nowhere near to being addressed.

Sadly, the victims must be the ones to step up and demand more than just a prison sentence for criminals. Victims must expect those in authority to take a more pro-active role in changing the factors that lead to higher crime rates. Victims must refuse to be used to bolster politicians' political platforms. New laws, more prisons and tough sentences have done nothing to change the victims' communities. Let the politicians out in little hick towns, who don't really care about crime ridden communities, refrain from giving self-serving lectures on how people should live. The suffering in these communities is real and citizens are in need of real solutions. Until crime victims take this stance, politicians will continue to parade around as super-heroes at their expense.

There is one bright spot, however. One group of people who have done more work to bring down the murder rates than any politicians, and gotten absolutely zero credit, are the emergency room doctors. So often, people are saved from multiple gunshot wounds, that people take it for granted that not too long ago, a lot of these same shooting victims would have died. In order to honor these fine men and women who have saved the lives of countless victims, we need to acknowledge that the homicide rate is a false way to measure crime from year to year since it doesn't take into account the crucial role these emergency room personnel have played in bringing down the death toll. The most accurate way to measure the crime rate is by the number of shootings, rather than the number of deaths, because shootings reflect the number of times a life threatening criminal activity took place, whereas a homicide only measures when that same activity led to death. There are around 600 non-fatal shootings in Milwaukee each year to go along with the 100 plus homicides.

If those in the media have any respect for the outstanding job these emergency room personnel have done, they will acknowledge that we must now count shootings rather than homicides to more accurately reflect where we are, in comparison with crime rates in the past. I know that a lot of people in authority will be upset by this, since the public will begin to have a more realistic sense of the crime problem. Did you really believe some super-hero politician who wouldn't dare set a foot in these high crime areas would actually be the one responsible for bringing down crime rates by virtue of having a big mouth? Perhaps politicians believe that much like a comic book hero their special weapon is their pen and by simply passing another law, we'll all be saved.

We are no longer in a situation where we can afford to live in a fantasy world. It's time for truth to make a comeback. Giving credit to those who have been at the forefront of bringing down homicide rates across America is long overdue. By honoring those who work in emergency rooms, we can show that if you want to make a difference, you have to actually do a lot of hard work and maybe even get your hands dirty.

RAPPERS & POLITICIANS

The two greatest frauds by trade in America's history are rappers and politicians. Both groups have a disproportionate number of pseudo-revolutionaries and self-proclaimed tough guys. They both have delusions of grandeur and rely on the simple-minded nature of their audience to accept their boasts and lies without question. Despite the fact that these snakes are cast from the same mold, they pretend to be polar opposites and adversaries.

Let's talk about the tough guy bit that both groups love to play. Is anyone really impressed by a self-proclaimed tough guy? For those of us that live in the real world and don't hide behind an army of bodyguards, nobody is tough. No neck has been made that can resist the bite of steel. Usually, when someone is doing all kinds of huffing and puffing about how tough they are, you can rest assured that they'd be the first ones to flee from the first sign of danger, or if cornered, soil their designer pants. Can you imagine any of these politicians meeting the criminals they want to be so tough on alone, somewhere secluded, and still running their mouth? They would quickly change their tune and be quite friendly and submissive. As to these tough rappers, they usually break down and rat on all their guys the minute they get into any serious trouble. A hot mouth should never be misconstrued as a sign of valor. What are their deeds? Getting shot? So if my house cat goes out and gets shot by some punk kid, he's now eligible to be a gangster rapper? The idea, fellows, is to avoid getting shot. I've known clowns in prison who'd been shot and liked to brag about it. The thing is, if you knew these guys you'd understand why someone would want to shoot them in the first place. It certainly wasn't because they were tough.

Regarding rappers and politicians being pseudo-revolutionaries, the reality is that both groups serve the status quo. The politicians do so in a more obvious fashion, claiming they'll be the ones to bring about the needed changes, while accepting millions in campaign contributions to keep the wheels greased for the powerful. The most amusing side-show has been the promise by politicians to change the culture. What makes politicians qualified to orchestrate a cultural revolution, is not something the media has bothered to ask. At the very least, these highbrow politicians should have been asked if granting people the gift of culture was in fact better than providing them with such things as affordable health care, good paying jobs, a clean environment, etc... Why bother with such trivial things though, when our leadership is fighting culture wars for us. Oh my!

Be not deceived, cultural revolutions occur as a result of social changes caused by inventions, discoveries, or works of art that by their magnitude, good or bad, force people to change how they perceive the world they live in, and therefore modify their behavior accordingly. For example, the Industrial Revolution in England resulted in a cultural revolution. Through each generation, much of the populace moved to the cities where the work was, which led the English people further and further away from the Puritanism of the previous era. What great works or inventions do our contemporary politicians offer us to change the culture? New Laws! Under that ideology, the ideal culture could only come to exist under a totalitarian regime, where the culture would be imposed by political leaders. That's what happened in Germany when Hitler was in power, and that's what's going on in North Korea today. In a free nation, culture is created by the people and reflected by the government, not the other way around! The quick fix of passing laws to change cultural problems demonstrates a complete ignorance of culture's role in a free society.

Meanwhile, the rapper parades around as a revolutionary, opposed to the government and politicians, voicing dissent over their oppression and folly, giving hope for glory to the unfortunate black youth. Deception, ignorance and bondage! Realize that politicians, especially Republicans, could dream of no greater gift than rappers as a propaganda machine to show the public why they want all these laws, cops, and prisons. Politicians and racists could never portray black people in the manner that rappers do with such evil tact as to glorify abusing women, using and selling drugs, and committing acts of violence like battery and murder. While politicians and racists publicly ridicule rappers, in private they would kiss them on the mouth for the job they've done. The racists are obviously delighted to see rappers encouraging the self-destruction of their own race, especially the youth. Pat yourselves on the backs, morons! You're doing a great job as the mouthpiece for the KKK.

Despite America's imperfections, if a child stays in school, avoids crime, and tries their hardest to succeed within the framework of the system, that child has as much if not more of an opportunity than do most of the world's children at living a decent life. The rappers who encourage children to buck the system are not only not giving the system a chance to work, but more importantly they are not giving the children a chance to be successful. This should not be surprising since without rap, most rappers would be failures themselves. For most Americans, the biggest obstacle they will face in their life is their self. If you avoid shooting yourself in the foot by getting into drugs and crime, your chances for success are pretty good.

When rappers glorify drug use, they are in collusion with drug dealers who trick children to use or sell drugs for them. The use of children in drug dealing has been a standard practice in our nation for a very long time. This is caused by the adult drug dealers being too cowardly to face the risk of incarceration for themselves and finding it much easier to manipulate kids to take all the risks for them. I equate these drug dealers who use children in this manner with pedophiles. When caught, they should be classified as child predators and not be allowed around children when released, just as if they'd raped a child. Make no mistake, the child who uses and sells drugs has been damaged for life in a manner similar to a child who has been molested. Drug using and dealing can lead to both physical and mental trauma to a child, which they might never recover from. Once these predators and their rapper accomplices that glorify drugs get these children hooked on drugs, it will be very difficult for that child to recover and fully realize their potential. Prisons and graveyards are full of young people whose talents will never come to light. The cost to society of the tragedies that inevitably follow when children get into drugs, tarnishes all the "bling-bling" that rappers like to show off from promoting that lifestyle. The ideology rappers promote to get their thirty pieces of silver is what's behind the destruction of our nation's cities. There could be no greater "Sell Outs!".

Obviously, rappers didn't invent all the wickedness that they glorify. However, unlike politicians, they do have an impact on the culture. They do help mold the perception of many of our nation's youth and with that comes a tremendous responsibility. The sad thing is that most of them are not even cognizant of the role they play. Yet, while politicians remain impotent at changing our culture, they have passed a number of laws resulting in our nation's prison population growing from one to two million people in recent years. This backlash to crime could not have happened, nor the entire Republican revolution of the 1990's, without the image of the "thug" being glorified so prominently by so called "gangster" rappers. For every dumb kid that thought it was cool, there was a multitude of horrified adults who flocked to the polls and voted en masse, which helped give the Republicans Congress in 1994.

Talk is cheap, and if a person can get away with talking instead of working, they'll usually take the easy way. Living in a democracy, freedom cuts both ways. People are free to lie about who they are or what's best for the country. It's up to the individual to be smart enough to not get conned. Politicians claim that what's best for the country is to become a police state with more cops and prisons. Rappers would have you believe that life is about getting high and accumulating money and "bitches," by any means necessary. If you look deep enough, you'll see that rappers and politicians are cut from the same cloth. Toilet paper. Maybe that's why they are so full of shit.

INDIVIDUALISM VERSUS COLLECTIVISM

Liberals generally support a collectivist approach in creating economic policies. The government taxes more in return for a larger safety net. The rationale for their economic view is that because we live in a prosperous society that gives us the opportunity to make such a good living, we should have no problem giving a little more back to help the underprivileged. Furthermore, if the economy collapses, there will be sufficient government programs in place to keep us from falling into a state of extreme poverty.

The conservative approach to economics places a greater emphasis on the individual. Their belief is that if you cut government programs and decrease taxes, you will stimulate the economy and create a less likely chance of economic depression. The conservative position is that because we live in a society with so much opportunity, if you can't succeed it's because of a lack of self-motivation. Furthermore, if more government help is given, that will only encourage people to be lazy and live off of other taxpayers.

For the most part, Americans tend to agree with the conservatives' more cynical, individualistic approach. One force that caused many Americans to have this view was the fact that America was not as dependent on the world economy as other countries. If you look at Scandinavian countries, where they traditionally provide a much greater safety net, those countries are much more affected by the global economy. Therefore, it's logical that people in those countries would want that type of protection.

In the past, when the global economy turned sour, America did have the resources to adopt an isolationist position until the global situation got better. I'm not sure this is as true today as in the past. As industrial jobs have left America, so have many of the skills. We don't have the same work force that we did twenty years ago. The next global recession might change the perception of Americans towards the idea of a safety net, albeit too late to save millions of Americans from the extreme poverty that they will experience in that situation.

There is some truth that when you try to help people, some will take advantage. However, this idea that you have to pull yourself up by the bootstraps, whatever that means, is fairly patronizing. People do have to be motivated to make things happen, but did Bush get into Yale, or the White House, on merit?

America has an infrastructure that creates the opportunity for success. Whether it's using public universities to get an education, roads to move the products you sell, or police and firefighters to provide safety to businesses from robbery and fire, everyone's success is possible because of the larger context within which they operate. Nobody is bigger than that.

Taxes are what allow us to maintain this infrastructure. The question is, how much to tax? We do have to consider the overall economic situation and be careful not to overtax. However, it's not about making as much money as possible now. If the current economy does great at the expense of the economy down the road, that's not a smart trade off. We must tax to the degree that we provide the next generation with the same opportunities and infrastructure that we have. This is not an easy policy decision to make and we need to elect leaders that are up to the task.

The way elections are currently held in the United States is insane. The constant use of emotional topics like crime, abortion and gay marriage, can only happen in a poorly educated society. An educated populace realizes that their government is like a huge multi-national corporation that they all own stock in. When we elect a president, we should be looking for the best C.E.O. around, and our Congressmen should be the best corporate board we can find. Trillions of dollars are at stake.

Since the government's main job consists of passing bills that spend our money, the main issue during an election should be how our money is being spent. The current team should have to defend the spending they voted for, while the challengers should present ways to change that dynamic. If they claim to want tax cuts, they should explain where they'd cut spending. If they think we should run a surplus or deficit, they should state their position on that. Every candidate should have a pie chart next to their name showing where they think the government should spend our money.

Once elected, compromises have to be made and politicians might not be able to get some of the spending changes they're for, implemented. However, let's at least know where people really stand with our money and what direction they want to go in. That way the people will have some idea of how their vote will influence how their money is spent. Some of the politicians, who usually just toe their party line, might have to give this issue some thought.

Individualism and collectivism are not limited to economics. Ironically, both parties flip roles when it comes to how to promote morality in our society. Liberals take the more individualistic approach. If you're not breaking the laws or hurting anyone, what you do is a matter of private conscience. The conservatives feel that since society does play such a large role in influencing people's behavior, moral values need to be taught by every institution, especially the government. Therefore, everything should be done to make the laws reflect their moral values.

Whatever way our society leans will impact how young people's identities evolve. The more individualistic people are, the more self-centered they'll be. The more collectivist they are, the more group oriented they'll be. We don't want a society full of narcissists or sheep.

Individualism is the finding of your identity through personal attributes while focusing on pursuing personal interests. This is fine, when balanced with finding your identity through social learning. Social learning emphasizes what society's interests and attributes are. Learning about your wants and needs has to be balanced with learning about society's wants and needs. Our well-being is dependent on society. Therefore, an understanding of society and its rules should not only be common knowledge, but it should also impact what type of person people choose to be.

When individualism is emphasized to the extreme, people assume that their thinking is more important than what society thinks. They believe that they can make up their own rules. This is extremely dangerous. Especially when drugs and guns are readily available to the youth who are constantly bombarded with this ideology.

In Dostoevsky's *Crime and Punishment*, the character Raskolnikov dreams about a world in which everyone believes that they are extraordinary people. The result is social chaos and people killing each other everywhere. Extreme individualism can blind people to the rights of others. This attitude is becoming more prevalent in America today. If we compare ourselves only to our own standards, it is easy to deceive ourselves that we are something greater than we are. To see others and ourselves as we are, rather than as we wish that we were, is important because by pretending to be more than we are, we become less than we ought to be. When we deny our human nature, which includes our imperfections, we dehumanize ourselves and others.

Individualists might argue, "What would happen if everyone had to wear the same clothes, drive the same car, etc…?" Then the individualist would claim that because we believe in rights, we believe people are responsible enough to have rights. Therefore, freedom is dependent on the assumption that people are responsible. However, the reality is that people are often irresponsible. Therefore, freedom is not absolute. A line has to be drawn which will protect freedom by limiting it because irresponsibility is a threat to freedom. That line must be drawn very carefully, recognizing both the responsibility that rights are dependent on, as well as the irresponsibility that is in human nature.

If we don't start with the right perspective on the issue of rights, we will not come up with the right answers. The individualist is dangerous in the rights debate because they will focus too intently on self-interests. For example, individualists might say they smoke marijuana responsibly, therefore marijuana should be legal. Individualists might also argue that alcohol and cigarettes cause more deaths than marijuana. However, they have failed to take into account all the people who use marijuana irresponsibly and how many deaths would be caused by marijuana if it were legal.

The collectivists are also dangerous because they focus too intently on the collective good without realizing that the collective good is dependent on the individual good. The collectivist would probably want to ban cigarettes, alcohol and marijuana. This would show a lack of understanding of human nature and would create more problems than it would solve. The collectivist would draw the line too strictly, while the individualist would draw the line too liberally. Either way, freedom is jeopardized.

When looking at whether marijuana, if legalized, would cause more of a loss of freedom than a gain of freedom, we must take into account what freedoms already exist and what loss of freedom those freedoms have caused. It's quite clear that alcohol and cigarettes are used irresponsibly at times, and therefore they may violate other people's freedoms. The question isn't what ill effects would the legalization of marijuana have, but rather what would be the ill effects of having marijuana, alcohol and cigarettes made legal?

By having too many freedoms, which in turn violate others' freedoms, you run the danger of backlash. This is because while everyone might have the right to use alcohol, marijuana and cigarettes, not everyone will exercise those rights. People who don't exercise those rights will be more prone to accept the collectivists' point of view. Too many freedoms alienate too many people. To decrease the possibility of a backlash against freedom, we limit what freedoms people have.

The individual should be respected in society. However, society is made up of a lot of individuals, therefore the individual can only be respected to a degree. Respect for the individual should not be greater than the respect that should be given to society as a whole. A society that places individuals' goals above those of society is embracing a self-destructive culture. Where you will find individualism the most damaging is in Corporate America. For the profit of a few individuals, we have often allowed companies to emit pollutants that have done significant damage to the environment, that the rest of society needs to survive. Again, for a campaign contribution, our politicians have ignored this abuse.

The debate over where we should draw the line between individualists and collectivists is in large part a debate over freedom. One must have a real understanding of what freedom consists of, to understand and argue this issue. Freedom is a duty. It is a duty for an individual to achieve their greatest potential. To merely use freedom to justify serving one's own self-interest is not to be free. A person who uses freedom to justify making bad choices for themselves, such as a glutton, a drug addict, an alcoholic, or a sex addict, is not free. They are all slaves of their desires. So, a free person without any productive goals is not free.

Many people get out of prison, and they feel that now that they're free they can do as they please. By not recognizing the responsibility to themselves and society that comes with this freedom, they immediately turn themselves over to a new master, drugs, alcohol, sex., etc....

It's hard for people not to be slaves to someone else's concept, if they have no concept of their own. Our society has multi-billion dollar industries that try to associate freedom with their product, and obviously they are very successful. This is because while the constitution is supposed to guarantee freedom, it can not guarantee what you choose to do with that freedom. For example, if you think that you're free because you bought some dope, alcohol, a tattoo, or even a motorcycle, you've got life messed up. A sucker can never be free.

Since both parties flip sides on the individualist-collectivist debate, they should have empathy for each other's position. While drawing the line in the economic debate is difficult, it is even more complex in moral-cultural issues. That is the area where politicians have less control, and perhaps why that debate is usually much more heated. Yet, it's not the people having the debate that are the problem. They are intelligent enough to see the pitfalls of each other's perspectives. It's that large section of society that doesn't even know a debate is taking place, much less what's at stake, that we should worry about.

A SCHIZOPHRENIC SOCIETY

While there are different types of schizophrenia, a schizophrenic disorder is marked by disordered thoughts, emotions, and communication. Our society is much the same way. On the one hand, our media glorifies violence, drug use, sex, profanity, and just about anything else that has to do with breaking the rules. On the other hand, our government, religious institutions and some media act with shock when people actually engage in these behaviors that are being glorified.

How did our society come to develop this personality? While frustrating, this inconsistency is the price you pay for living in a free country. America's history began as a rebellion. It's in the nature of the populace to test the limits of any authority that manifests itself, even moral authority.

For blacks, who didn't begin to obtain freedom until 1865, and then only in stages throughout another century, rebelling can be very tempting. When one rebels for so long to obtain freedom, it comes to a point where one cannot feel free without rebelling. Freedom and rebellion become a tandem. While this is true for all Americans, it is even more true for black Americans. Am I saying that black people are rebellious? Yes, and they should be!

Many people will think this is some sort of racist statement and will not be able to get past that. The reality is that by acknowledging that there are historical reasons for blacks to feel rebellious, we take a first step in addressing a bigger issue. How do you take those feelings and apply them constructively. We know how those feelings can be applied destructively, as half the nation's prison population is black, even though they're only twelve percent of the overall population.

Besides blacks, there are a lot of other rebels in prison too. America seems to have more rebels than any other country. Again, some of this can be traced back to history. Many Europeans came to America because they were oppressed in the countries they came from. Native Americans, Latinos and Asians each have their rebels too, and for different historical reasons. Recognizing these rebellious tendencies and directing those energies in a more pro-active manner would greatly reduce our prison population.

When a person feels that they are being degraded, by people or institutions, it is natural to resist that degradation in any way possible. Sometimes that degradation is so powerful and overwhelming that it blinds us, making us lash out in frustration. That is where we can get into trouble, as when we lash out, we tend to harm ourselves. There has to be a vision, or a dream, something to hold onto and guide us. Realizing that vision or dream is key, for success is the greatest rebellion there is.

One tool of rebellion that has been used both positively and negatively over the years is art. Art reveals many things. The more complicated the form, the deeper the facets can be cut. What we see in a work of art can be affected by the context in which we view it or the depth of our perspectives. Art is like a prism. Where you stand, and what way the light hits it, will determine how it is perceived. Good art has the potential of being comprehended in many different ways.

To understand the significance of art, one must differentiate between high art and low art. High art comes from high culture and therefore focuses on the natural world, humanity or the divine. A society that has a healthy culture will produce art that explores this wide spectrum with the purpose of uplifting, enlightening and exploring the depths of our understanding of both the physical and metaphysical universe.

Low art glorifies all that is crude. To understand it, one would have to look at the low culture from which it emanates. Low culture consists of a limited view of what life is really about. This shallow perspective allows whole societies to believe that the goals of life revolve around self-aggrandizement and self-pleasure.

Porn is obviously a low art form. Television and music have in recent years fallen pretty low. Where high art addresses issues of the heart, mind and soul, low art wallows in the bowels and groin. Low art is for the immature and underdeveloped person and society. For an adult, sex is not as significant as our contemporary media would indoctrinate us to believe. When adults sit down to talk, they discuss business, politics, religion, and maybe even sports. When young boys talk, it's all about the novelty of the idea of having sex. As an adult, this idea is no longer novel, and nothing to really brag about. Our media is run by little boys with little imaginations. They have no concept of what heights we could attain if they'd just make the effort to grow up.

As low art consistently dominates our media, our culture suffers. The minds of boys are never developed to maturity and therefore never expand past the middle school level topic of procreation. You expect to lead the world with this culture?

Perhaps into remission. Values underlie art and therefore much can be told about both a person and a society by the art they produce.

The challenge for the artist in modern times is to rise above the mass produced media and create something that will make their audience think, and hopefully on a topic of some importance. However, this might not be the most commercial thing to do. Low art outsells high art in societies with low culture, but there is still a market for high art.

Some people will mistake my position and claim that I'm being a prude. They would have people believe that being vulgar is sophisticated in that it shocks people. Foolishness. Sex, the body, vulgarity, all of that and much more can be addressed in high art. It's the concept, focus and method in which it's depicted that makes the difference.

In appraising art, one has to examine the message. For example, a tagger thinks his graffiti is a great work of art. While the graffiti could superficially be beautiful, the underlying message is ugly: that the artist has no respect for other people's property rights.

When huge profits can be made by creating art forms such as movies, music, books, magazines, even video games, that promote a low culture, we should not be surprised that so many people are willing to do so. Since we realize that the cost of consuming this garbage is the decadent, crime ridden society we have, why aren't Americans willing to elevate their tastes to a higher form of entertainment? This is one of the great failures of our educational system. In a prosperous society where much time and money are spent on leisure, it's crucial that people use this blessing wisely.

The government is in a very frustrating situation. They must suppress the behaviors that our media glorifies every day in countless ways. Religious leaders and parents also face a challenge in promoting morality in such a hostile atmosphere. Our institutions are clearly in a state of disorder.

People will probably mock the idea that the medication I prescribe for our nation's schizophrenia is more arts. Yet, I've seen people who have made dramatic changes as a result of art. It's very therapeutic and I would make art a part of any rehabilitation program, especially writing. Good art cannot be produced by an uneducated mind. When people get into arts, they are required to examine what beliefs they hold and why. Then, to express those beliefs, an artist must have a concept of their environment and their relation to it. This is where character and personality become refined.

In order to acquire a taste for high art, or develop the potential to create it, one must regularly sample it. A person that spends all their days watching porn on the Internet would probably have a hard time digesting Mozart's "The Magic Flute." Just as if I hadn't eaten meat in a year, and then tried to devour a big T-bone steak, my stomach might not appreciate it. The finer things take time, they need to be developed and we owe this to ourselves and to our society.

JUVENILE SUFFRAGE

Would allowing juveniles the right to vote benefit society? Most likely they would be heavily influenced by their parents. Still, there is a strong possibility that they would bring something new to the political landscape. Advertisers focus a lot on juveniles because they know they have a lot of disposable cash. Since money is the mother's milk of politics, you would soon see politicians pandering to this demographics' interest. Would George W. Bush have been so willing to execute a juvenile as Governor of Texas if he'd known he'd lose this demographics' votes when he ran for president? It certainly would have been considered.

Unless you would rather live in a "hypocrisy" than a democracy, the rights that we grant juveniles should not be based on political convenience. If a juvenile is considered mature enough to suffer the same, or more, criminal liability than an adult for their actions, then they should certainly be afforded the opportunity to participate in such a harmless venture as voting. Perhaps, by allowing this participation, juveniles might become more socially conscious and lessen, at least for some, their willingness to participate in criminal activities. Much of juveniles' desire to participate in things like drinking, drug use and cigarette smoking, comes from a misguided perception of what it is to be an adult.

It doesn't help when self-serving politicians term their rationalization for waiving juveniles into adult court by saying, "Adult punishments for adult crimes!" What is so adult about the commission of any crime? To the mature mind, which excludes many politicians, crime is the reflection of an immature mind. It is the inability of a person to function to a satisfactory degree in an adult world that causes them to resort to criminal activities. Juveniles who are trying to be adults before their time, and try to live as adults, often find that they're not ready. Males especially, who culturally are expected to be the bread winners, experience a great degree of frustration when they fail to succeed. A male from a poor family is going to feel a lot of pressure to make money at an early age and that is what tempts many young men to deal drugs. So, is committing a crime a mark of maturity? Of course not. The more immature a person is, the more vulnerable they are to being tempted to engage in criminal activities.

Recently, the Supreme Court decided we shouldn't execute juveniles any more because science now tells us what we knew for ages by common sense, that the juvenile brain is not fully developed. This is a step towards facing the facts. Consistency is the hallmark of a developed legal system. We should either consistently treat juveniles as adults by letting them vote, or always treat them as the children that they are by not waiving them into adult court.

If a juvenile can be treated as an adult when they're bad, then the same should apply when they are good. A juvenile who breaks the law can enter into the only enforceable legal contract, without the consent of their parent, that exists under the law—a confession! Since the reasoning for allowing these legal consequences is purely political, it is only fair that juveniles of an age eligible for waiver should be allowed to enter that political process and be given the right to vote.

Let's look at the contractual aspect of confessions. When entering into a contract, the terms of the contract must be specified in writing to ensure the validity of the contract. For example, when you get an offer in the mail for a credit card, you'll find all kinds of conditions of the terms of credit, albeit often in very small print, on the paper that they want you to sign and send back to them. They don't call you over the phone and give you this information orally and say, "If you want a credit card, just send us a letter saying you want a credit card and sign it, we'll worry about little details like interest rates later."

This is how we operate our legal system. When a suspect is asked to enter into a contract that could forfeit their life, or at least a good chunk of it, the law only requires that they be told briefly what rights they have. So, the laws for entering contracts are very different when it's the government trying to get something out of a suspected criminal. Why not have the same standard of protection for suspected criminals that we have for everyone else in society? Is getting a credit card a more serious affair than making a statement that could, in some cases, wrongfully put them in prison forever? Now, add the fact that a juvenile is not allowed under any circumstances to enter into a contract without the consent of a parent, much less a contract where the terms are issued orally and the consequences are not known until sentencing, it is obvious that the state's willingness to enforce these contracts is purely political. Yet what power advocates or legislates on behalf of juveniles?

Once waived into adult court, the idea that a juvenile could have an impartial jury is laughable. The jurors' awareness that a juvenile has been waived means that a judgment has been made by a judge that in order to give the juvenile a more severe punishment, he must be tried in adult court. Therefore a court has made a sentencing consideration pre-trial. Usually matters of sentencing are reserved for after a defendant is convicted, but not for juveniles. So much for the presumption of innocence!

Is the juror going to accept the idea that a reasonable judge would place an innocent juvenile in the county jail with the most vicious criminals of our society unless they were guilty? That's what they would have to believe to lack prejudice regarding the juvenile's guilt. Furthermore, if the public believed it was innocent juveniles being sent to the county jails to await their trials, they would be shocked and outraged. Instead, there is an overwhelming consensus that juveniles should be waived. Waiver into adult court is an implication of guilt, which our legal political system will never acknowledge.

Waiver of juveniles is also justified under the false premise that they will be tried as adults. The political question of whether juveniles should be tried as adults is a false question, designed to oversimplify the issue and mislead voters. There is no standard for what an adult will get for a given crime. So, how can someone honestly say that a juvenile will be tried "as" an adult?

Usually, what determines the degree of punishment a criminal receives is the amount of information they can trade the prosecutor for a lenient sentence. Thus, one serial killer such as Sammy "The Bull" Gravano, does a short time in prison because he can snitch on John Gotti. Juveniles usually have not had that much experience as criminals and therefore have less information to trade for leniency. The result is that juveniles and adults who weren't involved in a criminal lifestyle, and just did something stupid, get more punishment than experienced criminals. The message of our legal system is either get into the criminal lifestyle all the way, or you'll get hammered by the system if you break the law. The gang members, who tell on each other more than anyone, couldn't come up with a better recruiting poster for young criminals.

"Prisons are no longer places where just 'well adjusted' offenders are placed. The courts are confining a new breed of 'offender'—the retarded, the mentally ill, the young delinquent now branded an adult by court fiat, the Aids patient, the geriatric prisoner, and now (in serious numbers), the DWI offender. Combine this new population with tougher sentencing practices and parole boards reluctant to release, and there is no doubt the characteristics of prison populations are changing rapidly," said Anthony P. Travisono.

For society, the consequences are obvious. By giving most of the breaks to felons more entrenched in the criminal lifestyle, the prisoners most likely to re-offend get released the soonest. No wonder we have a high recidivism rate in the United States, and this might be by design. There is a large number of interests who advocate the lock them up and throw away the key approach. High recidivism rates help reinforce the spin that this is the right policy.

No major city in the United States could have a functioning legal system without the plea bargain. When politicians scream about being tough on crime, what they really mean is being tough on high profile cases, people who are borderline retarded or just not criminally savvy, and juveniles. The easy cases go to trial, thus the high conviction rate for prosecutors at jury trials. This way they can brag about how good they are.

To be inconsistent in the way we deal with juveniles, due to political agendas, undermines the credibility of adult authorities in promoting any value system. At the very least, juveniles should not be doing more time than adults for the same, or even lesser crimes. The fact that it took our government so long to ban the death penalty for juveniles, shows that even when obvious wrongs are being done, no one in authority cares because there are no political consequences. To change that, juveniles should be given the right to vote.

CHICKENHAWKS

Many people think of Chickenhawks as pro-war politicians who have never served in the military. In prison, the term Chickenhawk has a different connotation. Just as the Chickenhawk swoops down on the barnyard in search of prey, the pedophile swoops down on the schoolyards in search of young children to molest. They stalk their prey until the object of their desire is vulnerable to attack. At that point, the thinking process ends, and their animal instincts take over. Both humans and birds are predators that act on impulse.

The prison system is full of Chickenhawks, who do sometimes travel in flocks. The sheer number of them is amazing. A lot of people have mislead the public about how hard prison is for these feathered freaks. It is thought that the other inmates will pick on them. This is part of the imagery of prison life sold to the public to make them feel good about their glorious, tough penal system.

Do Chickenhawks suffer from the lack of privacy in most prisons? Let us consider the communal showers that most prisons have. As perverts, Chickenhawks are generally not shy. The prospect of seeing a 16 or 17 year old boy waived into an adult prison, or even someone older who just looks younger, all soaped up and naked, is not a great punishment to our local Chickenhawk population. I suppose that's the state's idea of rehabilitation.

While rapes are rarer in prison than people think, I'm sure that after being eyed by a few Chickenhawks in the showers, these young lads feel violated. Even if they weren't touched, they might feel dirtier upon exiting the shower than they did upon entering. Keep in mind that the rest of the prisoners aren't even allowed to buy pornographic magazines to see pictures of nude, adult women. This, while Chickenhawks enjoy the shower scene, or if they get desperate, they have the children's section of a JC Penney's catalog to serve their evil purpose. Are Chickenhawks the ones being deprived?

Let us consider the job prospects for Chickenhawks in prisons. A big factor in how a prisoner does their time is if they are able to get a job during their incarceration. Mind boggling as it may seem, there are not a lot of jobs available for prisoners despite the fact that they only get between .25¢ and $1.00 an hour. I'm sure the Chinese would not allow such a cheap labor pool to go to waste, but in the land of massive government spending, our leaders can't figure out a way to tap into this resource. Forgive me for digressing, but the state of the Chickenhawks must be understood within the context of their habitat.

Two factors play a role in making Chickenhawks good candidates for jobs in prisons. The first is that Chickenhawks are not usually trouble makers. The second is that since you cannot expect a person that rapes children to have a concept of loyalty or honor, Chickenhawks have no problem snitching on their fellow inmates. Understand that guards often have to supervise large numbers of prisoners at a time. Having a good percentage of Chickenhawks that are well behaved, and will snitch on the others if they misbehave, makes things a whole lot easier for the guards. The only thing that might distract a Chickenhawk from doing their duty is if a young boy happened to drift through their work area. This is fairly unlikely.

This isn't to say that guards like or respect Chickenhawks, it's just easier for them to take the path of least resistance. This is also the reason the vast majority of prisoners don't pick on Chickenhawks. The penalty for threats in a Wisconsin prison is 180 days in segregation. For cruelty to animals, fighting, or battery, the penalty is 360 days, plus a trip to Supermax if you're deemed too rebellious.

Now, make no mistake. You will do the entire punishment. They don't let you out early for good time, behaving, very often, because they've built so many lock-up cells that they struggle to keep them filled. Wisconsin inmates are fairly tame. That's why our Supermax was never more than half full, until they made one section into a regular maximum security prison. Imagine the stupidity of building a Supermax, the most expensive kind of prison, and leaving it half empty for years.

What prisoners in their right mind are going to subject themselves to all that time in the hole just to ruffle a few feathers on a Chickenhawk? In segregation, they leave the lights on all day and all night. You can't buy any food on canteen or have any property except a Bible, a dictionary, stamped envelopes, paper, a pen, an address book, 25 letters and legal papers. You only get two showers a week. Recreation consists of standing in a cage. After a couple of months, two on a 180 and four on a 360, you can get your TV and radio if you've been a good boy. The only books you'll see are those they hand out, which are not always very good and often have pages missing. No magazines or newspapers. I've personally seen people mentally deteriorate to the point of insanity in these conditions. Grown men painting the walls of their cells with their own feces. They are eventually put on some kind of medication. When they are released from prison, they live on SSI because they can no longer function to the degree where they'd be able to hold onto a job. Wisconsin has the highest suicide rate amongst prisoners in the nation. Perhaps other states' segregation units aren't as bad, although I'm sure they're close. Everyone's got to be tough on crime!

Each prison varies a little in its policies and procedures. For example, Oshkosh has a prison where they have a large section dedicated to rehabilitating sex offenders. If you say "tree jumper" or "Chickenhawk" in Oshkosh, you will get a ticket for disruptive conduct, which also carries 360 days in segregation. With all the power of the state behind them, you can understand why prisoners leave the Chickenhawks alone. When the Chickenhawks do get attacked, it's usually for running their mouth to the wrong person or not paying a gambling debt. In almost 17 years, I don't remember anyone ever being physically attacked for being a Chickenhawk. Jeffrey Dahmer doesn't count because from what I heard, he had called Scarver a porch monkey. I also heard that Scarver covered his face with toothpaste as if it were war paint when he attacked. Either way, a Chickenhawk being attacked is a rare sight in nature.

In Wisconsin, former Governor Tommy G. Thompson is highly revered among Chickenhawks. He not only got Supermax built, but also some very large segregation units in Waupun and Green Bay. With the safety of the Chickenhawks insured, they could fly high in Wisconsin's prison system. In the old days, Chickenhawks were much quieter and more humble. Now that they feel protected, as though they were under the Endangered Species Act, they've become quite bold and walk around preening and screeching as if they owned the joint.

You can imagine how disgusted the rest of the inmates are by this development. The irony is how the public rejoiced when these prison beds were added, as though the salvation of the world depended on it. They might as well have made signs saying, "Save the Chickenhawks," and marched on Madison because that's all that was accomplished. So, the next time you hear someone say how rough it will be for the Chickenhawks, think again. They love this environment. Why else would sex offenders have the highest recidivist rate of all criminals?

GOVERNMENT WASTE

The American legal system has a number of areas where waste is prevalent. When millions of dollars are spent each year, you'd think someone would start asking some questions to see if all this spending is really necessary. Once upon a time, there were journalists, and they asked a lot of questions. Today, questioning authority is not what polite journalists do. After all, if a journalist were to make someone look bad, they might not be given that exclusive interview or dinner invitation. Since I don't expect any dinner invitations, I'm not going to worry about stepping on anyone's toes.

One of the first things that should be eliminated is the practice of giving just about every criminal defendant a psychological evaluation. Attorneys should be commended for wanting to thoroughly investigate the potential defense claims for their clients. However, when most defendants are going to cop a plea, it's an incredible waste of money to pay psychologists with tax dollars to evaluate these people for nothing. Part of this is the fault of the prosecutors, who often act wishy-washy and don't make a plea offer until months have passed. The defense attorney doesn't know if the case is going to trial and therefore he has to prepare the case accordingly.

The way a District Attorney should run things is within two weeks of arrest, they should offer a plea bargain, if that's what they are going to do. Some D.A.s would say that's not enough time. Bull! If you know enough to charge someone with a crime and put them in jail, you'd better know the facts of the case.

After the plea is offered, the defendant would have another two weeks to determine whether or not to take the deal. If they take the deal, that saves all the money the county would have spent on the public defender for preparing the case, the psychologist for the mental evaluation, and housing the inmate in the County Jail for sometimes over a year. The whole reason for giving a deal is to save money, yet by letting the case drag on for months, taxpayers are paying a lot more than they should. If the defendant doesn't take the deal in two weeks, the plea bargain should be off the table. Everyone who lives in a major city should be demanding that type of efficiency from their D.A..

If a defendant chooses not to take the plea, it should still not be automatic that they get a psychological review. If they have no history of mental health problems, and they are not claiming the reason they committed the crime was due to mental illness, then the defense counsel should not be expected to explore this potential defense any further. Only if a defense counsel feels there is a realistic chance for an insanity claim to be made, should they proceed with the evaluations. Millions of these evaluations are being done each year, just so defense attorneys can claim they've covered all the bases.

When the Court orders a psychological evaluation, psychologists are chosen based on whose evaluations the D.A. and the defense attorney liked in the past. They often object to each other's selections and sometimes, if there is no compromise, the Court will order multiple examinations. Clearly, if you're a psychologist and you like a steady check from the state to supplement your income, it would be best to consistently tailor your conclusions so that they are either for or against the defendant. This isn't to say that all psychologists do this, but acting as a professional when working with our illustrious legal system could result in fewer requests by prosecutors or defense attorneys for your services.

The kicker is that in the rare case when a not guilty due to insanity plea is actually raised by the defendant, it has a less than one percent chance of being successful. Even though the insanity defense is written in the state's statutes regarding defenses to criminal liability, most prosecutors treat the claim as though it were some form of scam. Consequently, many jurors are skeptical of this defense and view it as a way of getting away with crime.

Spending one's life in a mental institution is better than life in prison, but not by much. In some cases, the insanity defense is used by defense attorneys because they couldn't figure out anything else to raise as a defense. It is often the defense of last resort. The abuse of this defense, by attorneys who use it just because it's there, and prosecutors who belittle it as a scam, results in a lot of crazy people in prison. That makes it difficult for prison staff, who aren't trained to deal with the mentally ill, and usually makes the mentally ill's condition worse by the time they're released.

If you eliminate all the bogus evaluations and cut down on the abuse in using this defense, we actually might have a chance of addressing mental illness in our legal system. When crazy people get out of prison, ugly things can happen. Prosecutors should really not be so dismissive of this defense. Public safety is at stake here and when mentally ill people get out of prison and snap, victims' families should demand to know why nothing was done to treat these people. Usually, the first time mentally ill people come through the system they have done something foolish, but not necessarily violent. That's a red flag to deal with the problem. Considering what's spent on psychologists, you'd think we'd be making some progress in this regard. The inefficiency in the way cases are managed eliminates that possibility however.

Another wasteful by-product of our legal system is the pre-sentence investigator. In cases where a plea bargain has been made, it defies logic to pay someone to do what amounts to a background check when the outcome has already been determined. That's like hiring someone for a job and then doing a background check. Once the plea bargain is agreed to, there need not be all this fluff to rationalize why the agreement was made.

As to the judge, he is not bound to go along with the plea agreement. In other words, the judge could disregard the deal and sentence a defendant to the maximum sentence anyway. However, doing that would severely undermine the system's ability to function. Judges go along with plea deals to save the taxpayers' money. The pre-sentence investigator's recommendation really doesn't mean much. There are plea deals where the prosecutor stands silent on the recommendation or gives a broad recommendation, like from five to ten. So that's the justification to spend all this money? Get a spine, prosecutor! Make a specific recommendation and be done with it. Quit worrying about running for election down the road.

The recommendation of a pre-sentence investigator is even less relevant in a case that goes to trial. They do not attend the trial, yet we pay them to make recommendations to the judge, who should have been watching the trial, on how much time someone should get. That's like if we had the judges in an ice skating competition refer to the recommendation of people who didn't even watch the skating. Would any judge of any worth pay attention to that recommendation? Ice skating is far too serious to allow such foolishness, but not our legal system. Furthermore, the defense attorney and prosecutor, who also attended the trial, are paid to make recommendations on how someone should be sentenced.

People might think it's good for the defendant to have this pre-sentence investigator find reasons for why they committed their crime. That's what the trial was for! Generally, the pre-sentence investigator takes their cue from the prosecutor. That's the first person they talk to about what happened, and since the defendant was found guilty, that's the version they'll go along with. It is extremely rare that a pre-sentence investigator makes a recommendation closer to the defense attorney' recommendation than the prosecutor's. Do we really need to pay someone a salary to cosign the prosecutor? They don't have enough juice in the courtroom?

Since there is no constitutional requirement for a pre-sentence investigator, the claim that this expense is necessary is a fraud, from the legal standpoint. While judges probably wouldn't admit it, I wouldn't be surprised if many didn't even bother to read the pre-sentence investigator's report. I'm sure it's nice to have a cushy job where you recommend a number, and even if nobody ever followed your advice, it wouldn't matter. A defendant isn't entitled to any relief if the pre-sentence investigator's report was wrong, the judge would simply say he didn't base the sentence on that, which he probably didn't. What's at stake? Nothing. That's why the position of pre-sentence investigator should be eliminated from the English language. If thirty years from now people hear pre-sentence investigator and ask, "What's that?" my life will have been a success.

I'm glad we have a system that likes to spend money. I'm glad defense attorneys are willing to leave no stone unturned. Some defendants like having a pre-sentence investigator come and talk to them while they await sentencing, especially if it's a she and she is good looking. The problem is that inefficiency doesn't benefit the defendants or the taxpayers. If all pre-sentence investigators were laid off and psychological evaluations were only done in cases that were going to a jury trial, and then only if the defense attorney thought the insanity defense had real potential, hundreds of millions of dollars would be saved. That's a worthy topic of discussion.

PRISON P.T.S.D.

One of the most traumatic and stressful situations a person can experience is incarceration. Even if you don't get beaten or raped, the constant stress of dealing with hostile people, whether inmates or guards, will build up to a breaking point over the years. This can be manifested by a nervous breakdown or the development of a personality disorder.

During incarceration, there are no breaks, no days off, and there is no time given to recuperate your sanity. Even if you go to solitary confinement, that is typically the loudest area in the prison. In many instances people are doing 10-20-30 years at a crack. It is no wonder that when some people get out of prison they literally snap.

Though not news worthy, and therefore escaping the public's attention, prisoners often snap before they even get out of prison. Since no guns are available, some inmates fire urine and feces at guards. This almost always happens in segregation. I've never seen it anywhere else. Since segregation is the most stressful environment in the prison, this should not be a surprise.

Where is the psychologist that is going to stand up to their employer, the Department of Corrections, and tell them that instead of punishing inmates even more when they have a mental breakdown, they should try to avoid creating such a stressful environment that leads to these episodes in the first place? However, most people don't care how unruly inmates are treated in their prisons, especially if they've done something to "justify" that treatment. This isn't to say that prisoners don't get psychiatric care in prison. The problem is that there is very little effort to alleviate the stress that is the cause of so many psychological problems. Then add the fact that upon release, psychiatric care is unavailable for most ex-convicts.

I guess the question is why should anyone, including the psychiatric community, care about how stress affects felons during and after incarceration? If psychiatry is to have any credibility, it must be consistent in the application of its diagnoses. For soldiers who return from the horrors of war, there is sufficient political capital to allow society to have empathy when veterans engage in some unordinary and sometimes criminal behavior. This often falls under the category of Post Traumatic Stress Disorder, P.T.S.D..

Imagine the psychiatric community trying to apply this same argument to ex-convicts, who in some cases have gone through as much or worse horrors in America's prisons? Most men would probably prefer taking the risk of being shot than that of being raped. Still, I will not trivialize the stress of war to prove that prisoners undergo a great degree of stress. War and incarceration are opportunities for stress to have their greatest impact because the person experiencing them can't just walk away when they've had too much. Escape and desertion are both crimes taken very seriously by our government.

Is there a correlation between stress and a person's behavior? It is well documented that a large number of soldiers and prisoners are prone to alcohol or drug dependency after doing time in a war zone or in a prison. Experiencing high levels of stress and trauma make a person susceptible to engage in activities that will help them escape the continued experience of that stress and trauma through their memory.

Even though the event is over, the human brain has the same stress reaction whenever a veteran or prisoner recalls their experiences. The pressure, frustration, anger, rage, conflict and anxiety all come flooding back. Doing drugs or drinking are ways people try to cope with that. Obviously, this opens the door for other problems.

Soldiers and prisoners often have the same feelings of powerlessness or helplessness that eat away at their psyche. Soldiers who are sitting ducks awaiting the justification to use force, which usually only comes after being attacked, slowly have their ego chipped away as their comrades are chewed up by improvised explosive devices and snipers. For soldiers, trained both physically and psychologically to be aggressive in the face of the aggressor, these continuous assaults without an opportunity to fight back can cause them to feel emasculated.

Prisoners who suffer from numerous forms of degradation, at the hands of both inmates and guards, can also feel emasculated by their experience. This can range from verbal to physical abuse. Then there's the aspect of dealing with an all powerful government that takes privileges away, based on the whim of a politician. The state is saying, "We're taking your cigarettes, cassette tapes, porn magazines, etc., because we can, punks!" Even more frustrating is when the government rejects valid appeals. Compared to the plight of the soldier, it's not as much of a physical grind. Over the long haul, the psychological result is the same, the feeling of emasculation.

Considering that most prisoners and soldiers value strength as an important character trait, the feeling of emasculation can lead to aggressive behavior as a way to compensate for this perceived degradation. When you add the aforementioned tendencies toward drug and alcohol abuse, you can end up with a powder keg ready to explode. Understanding this for both groups is important. The fact that there are so many people who are not aggressive by nature, and whom everyone got along with, who then undergo this dramatic character swing after going to war or prison, proves that stress has a negative impact on behavior. The greater the stress experienced, and the more prolonged the duration, the more likely a person will eventually react with some form of negative behavior.

The big difference between ex-convicts and veterans is that veterans have learned self-discipline as part of their training. This gives them a greater ability to self-regulate these tendencies, but it is not foolproof. Self-awareness goes a long way in controlling the self, however. Should we not then encourage both veterans and ex-convicts to seek the introspection found when receiving psychological treatment?

After a person has served in combat, it would be outrageous not to always offer free psychological care to that veteran for the rest of their life. Furthermore, there should be no social stigma attached to that treatment. It would be no different than getting treatment for a piece of shrapnel left in the body.

After serving time in prison, ex-convicts should also be eligible for free psychological care. It would be cruel and unusual punishment to subject a person to one of the most stressful experiences a human being can endure, and then kick them out on the streets with no resources to help them cope with what they've been through. This isn't about justifying or excusing failure, it's about understanding why people are failing so that we can do everything to prevent the next murder, robbery spree, or over-dose from happening. Realizing why a person is trying to destroy their self is a step toward treating them and preventing them from destroying others in the process.

Do criminals already have tendencies to engage in these behaviors, thus the reason for their being incarcerated in the first place? Of course, and they do bear the brunt of the responsibility to change. However, many of these people lack structure, and unless someone provides it to them, they will not have a platform to stand on from which to make those changes. Our prison system should not consistently make people who are bad, worse. The fact that this happens all the time should certainly be at the forefront of the debate of whether continuously increasing our prison population will in fact reduce the number of crimes, or their severity, in the long term.

RESTORATIVE JUSTICE

Restorative justice is a way of thinking about how we should deal with crime victims, criminals and the overall impact of crime on communities. The idea is that justice should be a process that victims, criminals and the community can participate in, while respecting the dignity of all parties. The process should bring about as much recovery as possible for the victim and community, while rehabilitating the criminal. That rehabilitation would include making reparation to the victim and community, while facing up to what they did and planning what they will do to avoid getting into trouble in the future.

The fact that restorative justice is a fairly novel idea shows just how estranged our system has gotten from a basic concept of justice. The system has focused on retribution, the punishment of criminals, at the expense of resolving the underlying causes of crimes. To do that, you have to deal with the relationships between the criminals, their victims and the community. In some cases, this is impossible due to the nature of the crime, but it's simply foolish to treat every criminal as a social pariah. All that does is guarantee that once a person has been through the system, they'll have difficulty functioning in a society that they have come to see as an adversary.

By nature, the American people are very forgiving. After World War II, the United States invested billions of dollars to rebuild Japan and Germany. This, despite the war crimes and terrible costs in both human and financial terms that the world incurred as a result of these nations' aggressions. How long did it take before Americans were buying German and Japanese products again? Germany's Volkswagen buses and bugs were quite popular in the 1960's. In the 1970's Toyota and Honda started making a name for themselves with their fuel efficient vehicles during the oil crisis. The war had just ended in 1945!

So, between 15 and 25 years was how long Americans held a grudge for Pearl Harbor, Aushwitz, the Bataan Death March, the Battle of the Bulge, etc… Whole books have been written on their war crimes. Yet, more criminals are executed each year in the United States than were hung after the Nuremburg trials. In comparison with some of the short prison sentences that war criminals were getting, today's American criminals are getting prison sentences that in some cases defy belief. How can a legal system give what amounts to life sentences for just about any crime imaginable?

In the case of World War II, it made sense to rehabilitate Germany and Japan. Their prosperity would help promote the overall prosperity of the world economy. Today, nobody would think twice of buying a BMW, or owning a Sony PlayStation. If we can realize that kind of potential overseas, what does it say about contemporary America that we can't see any potential amongst our own? Is it such a courageous act to throw away people's lives for a mistake?

The real test of a justice system is whether it's beneficial. Does it provide a working structure to solve a social problem? While we, imperfect beings that we are, will never be able to create a system that provides complete justice, we should always strive for that ideal. By being humble and understanding our limitations, we might come fairly close to providing the ideal atmosphere for a justice system to operate.

What we label our justice system, punitive or restorative, is not as important as the underlying attitude of those who are in authority and have the awesome responsibility of measuring out justice. At the same time, different systems have different benefits and we need to weigh the overall consequences of a system to determine if we need to make changes. However you want to categorize the current system, it doesn't seem to be working.

Since a justice system should address the wrong that one party has committed to another, an attempt should be made to right the wrong. The problem is that in most felonies the wrong can never be completely righted. This is because the experience that the victim went through can never be taken back, and the change in the victim's perceptions cannot be totally undone.

Attempting to undo what really can't be undone is frustrating. It's much easier to skip the idea of resolving a problem and using the punishment as a way to appear concerned about the victim. Justice has often been sold as a way to control or fix a situation. The quicker and easier, the better. There is no quick fix to crime however, and it is insulting to crime victims to pretend otherwise.

There are two options in life, conflict and resolution. One would have to live a very sheltered life not to experience some insult, outrage, provocation or crime every now and then. Do we deal with that by going to war? When it's a crime, do we want the government to go to war on our behalf? Some people do, and in some cases it's understandable due to the nature of the crime. Most of the time, it's not necessary to go that far. We can resolve a lot of problems without all the theatrics of our current system.

Justice acknowledges the importance of people and the value we place on their rights. Pursuing justice doesn't justify being destructive or cruel. Destroying people to show how much we value laws is a strange form of justice. A little restraint on the part of our government would go a long way towards restoring a justice system that benefits all parties.

REHABILITATION

Society is like an apple tree. Every year, the apple tree produces apples. Just as the apples grow and ripen on the tree, so do our youth grow and ripen in society. Just as the apple eventually comes off the tree, so does the youth have to eventually come out into society.

The problem is that some of the apples are not coming out right. These apples represent the criminals. Every year, there are more and more bad apples. The farmer sees this and separates the bad apples from the rest, just as society separates the criminals by incarcerating them.

The farmer realizes that whatever he does to the bad apples that have fallen off the tree, will not heal the tree, just as the punishment of the criminal doesn't address the root causes of crime. Being tough on criminals by throwing them away in prisons for lengthy periods would be the equivalent of a farmer throwing away the bad apples. The farmer is not so foolish however. He takes the bad apples and rehabilitates them by cutting out what is bad and using what's left to make apple sauce, pies, and jams. Humans are more complicated than apples and some will refuse to be rehabilitated. This does not justify failing to make a genuine effort, since the prospect of saving just one human being makes everything worthwhile.

The question of how we should treat criminals is as old as mankind. Alexis de Tocqueville wrote, "In the Middle Ages, when it was difficult to overtake offenders, the judges inflicted the most dreadful tortures on the few who were arrested, which by no means diminished the number of crimes. It has since been discovered that when justice is more certain and more mild, it is at the same time more efficacious."

If one is for or against rehabilitation, a rational debate on the topic can ensue. The problem with our legal system is that it hasn't fully committed to which side it is on. The government spends millions of dollars on rehabilitation programs in prisons every year. At the same time, some laws, and the attitudes of some in authority, are completely contrary to the idea of rehabilitation. The result is that the rehabilitation programs have become nothing more than a façade for leaders to hide behind, and pretend they're trying, while sandbagging the process for political reasons.

Imagine a group of people being told that they had to learn biology to succeed in society. On the first day of class, the group is told by the biology teacher that they are all scum. Then, on top of being scum, the first rule of biology is that everyone in the class is biologically incapable of learning biology. What do you think the success rate in that type of setting would be?

I'm not going to argue that some of the people sentenced to prison aren't scum. However, it is not beneficial or mature for judges and prosecutors to be insulting. The focus should be on what the defendant did, and that is where the shame should lie. Giving the news media a show is not the reason for a sentencing hearing. I understand that some cases are so outrageous that emotions will be difficult to hold in check, but judges and prosecutors need to act with a certain degree of professionalism and dignity.

One of the first things a prisoner looks into when they get to prison is what the criteria are for a time cut or sentence modification. Most states require that a prisoner show a "new factor" to get a sentence modification hearing. Without going too deep into the legal meaning of a new factor, it does not have anything to do with being rehabilitated. You can't go to Court and claim that because you got a college degree, did all your programs, behaved in prison, etc... that these are new factors for the judge to consider in determining their sentence. The reason is that when the judge originally sentences a defendant, they assume that the prison system is not an environment conducive to rehabilitation. Since rehabilitation is not a factor in the original sentence, it cannot be a new factor that would have changed their original decision. Prisoners are essentially being told by our laws that they are expected to fail. They are biologically incapable of learning.

In the past, the judge's refusal to consider rehabilitation was rationalized by the fact that the parole board would consider rehabilitation at the parole hearing. That was too much for former Wisconsin Governor Tommy G. Thompson to stand. In 1994, Thompson wrote to then Department of Corrections Secretary Michael Sullivan and told him,"I believe that mandatory release of violent criminals is wrong," and "I hereby direct the Department of Corrections to pursue any and all available legal avenues to block the release of violent offenders who have reached their mandatory release date." Obviously, if Thompson opposed mandatory release, he also opposed early parole. In 1994, 698 people were released on mandatory release, while 3,327 were paroled. By 2001, the number of mandatory released jumped to 4,131, while the number paroled dropped to 1,872.

When judges sentenced people under the old law, they considered the fact that a prisoner only had to do a quarter of their time before they had a parole hearing. If a judge wanted a felon to do 10 years, he would have given him a forty year sentence. The problem with that, is mandatory release on a forty year sentence, two-thirds, is almost twenty-seven years. So, if the policy of the Department of Corrections, which the parole board is part of, is to hold people as long as possible, the prisoner could end up doing close to three times as much as the judge intended. Thompson's directive circumvented the due process rights of prisoners, by eliminating a chance for a fair parole hearing. This is a classic example of what happens when justice becomes politicized.

After this directive, many of those that actually got paroled were only a few weeks or months from mandatory release! This was done so the state could say it was still paroling people. Clearly, the numbers show that over the years, despite a tremendous increase in the number of prisoners, the State has enacted a policy to keep as many parole eligible prisoners locked up as long as possible.

These prisoners who do all their programs, and then get denied parole over and over, and end up doing the same mandatory release as those prisoners who sat around doing nothing with their time, will naturally be resentful and bitter by the time they're released. That's a smart policy?!! Spend millions to rehabilitate them, then get them upset and frustrated by telling them that all those programs they took didn't mean anything, then let them out. This is the greatest country in the world!

This entire issue was rendered moot for prisoners who came in after "truth-in-sentencing" was passed. For those prisoners, politicians had completed the process of eliminating rehabilitation as a worthwhile goal. Under "truth-in-sentencing", a prisoner could complete every program imaginable and not be released one minute earlier than what their sentences dictated. Shouldn't taxpayers expect a return on the investment of paying for all these rehabilitation programs in prisons? Releasing prisoners earlier when they've shown a willingness to learn from their mistakes, would save taxpayers the tremendous cost of their continued incarceration. States with truth in sentencing evidently don't need to save that kind of money.

One of the reasons "truth-in-sentencing" was passed in many states was because the Federal Government provided funds to states that passed laws they liked. The Federal Government has gotten into the dirty habit of getting into the business of state legislatures. Legislation should be passed on behalf of the people of that state, not dictated by the Federal Government. Where are the conservatives to clamor against such an intrusion of state's rights? Woops! Actually they were behind truth in sentencing getting passed in this manner in the first place. State legislators are at fault for seeing nothing wrong with money dictating law. If the Federal Government is going to continue to bribe states to get the laws they want enacted, let's eliminate the burden of having a state legislature. We can let the fellows in D.C. make all our laws.

Clearly, there are a lot of powerful people opposed to having rehabilitation play any role in our system. They have decided to take the easy way out and give up on the lost sheep. Still, they present a formidable obstacle for those who'd like to change the system. Those who advocate rehabilitation must be realistic about what to expect from criminals if they hope to be successful.

There are some people who will come back to prison after their first time in, regardless of what type of system you have. Others are fortunate enough to have the support and character that enables them to make the changes that are necessary so they don't come back. The third group, which is the majority, consists of many young prisoners that don't really have a solid persona. They are malleable. These are the ones that have the greatest potential of being influenced, positively or negatively, during their first incarceration.

In order to have an influence on those that can be influenced, authority must appear legitimate in the manner they treat them. The sentence they receive, and the manner in which they are treated during that sentence, must be based on a set of principles that are applied equally to all people. Once the system is changed, so that how people are treated is based on a set of principles rather than on political ambitions, those people that can be influenced will no longer be burdened by the stumbling block of having to recognize the blatant inconsistency which our legal system is drowning in.

Our system focuses too much on control without understanding the importance of having influence. Authorities are unwilling to recognize the limitations of their control. No matter how much power they obtain, they will never be able to prevent people from choosing to break laws. The most that can be hoped for is to have a positive influence on people's decisions.

Why did society decide that the government, rather than the individual, should be the one to punish criminals? "Philosophers have debated the reasons for this transfer to government of the victim's desire to strike back at the offender. Henrich Oppenheimer lists several theories. Three of them are as follows: (1) In the theological view, retaliation fulfills a religious mission to punish the criminal. (2) In the aesthetic view, punishment resolves the social discord created by the offense and reestablishes a sense of harmony through requital. (3) In the expiatory view, guilt must be washed away through suffering. Ledger Wood advances a fourth explanation, a utilitarian theory. Punishment is considered to be a means of achieving beneficial and social consequences through application of a specific form and degree of punishment deemed most appropriate to the particular offender after a careful individualized study of the offender."

There are two purposes for incarceration. The first is to punish the individual who committed a crime. This is done to teach a lesson, not out of vengeance. The other purpose of incarceration is to keep society safe from someone who, in their present state, would be likely to repeat an offense. This is why rehabilitation is so important. If the state of a person's thinking isn't changed while they're incarcerated, that person will probably return to a life of crime when they are released.

When these two purposes for incarceration are disregarded by those in authority, they undermine the partial solution it is. The lesson that a person is supposed to learn from being incarcerated is that society is your friend, but because you have disregarded this friendship by committing a crime, you will be removed from society and put in prison. In prison, a person is supposed to learn that they reap what they sow. Planting bad seeds through drug and alcohol abuse, violence, greed, sloth, lust, etc… will result in a very sour harvest. Immoral behavior is not productive and therefore not beneficial to anyone.

People often commit crimes to solve their problems. People take drugs to escape from reality. People deal drugs or steal because they have a money problem. People kill people as a result of having people problems. Incarceration should teach criminals that everyone has problems, but you can't deal with your problems by committing crimes. If you do, you'll pay by going to prison.

Authorities often try to simplify this whole process into a matter of right and wrong. Being right about something is not always beneficial however. If in the process of being right we try to lord it over others and use it to justify cruelty or arrogance, then being right becomes being self-righteous. In any field, not losing sight of the objective is what separates the professionals from the amateurs. What's the big picture? While our system is full of self-righteous rhetoric, there is very little success to show for it.

The system must be designed to lead criminals to the right conclusions about themselves and society. That is why it's important not to violate criminals' rights and be unnecessarily harsh on them. Society needs to be recognized by the criminals as a friend, not as an enemy. This facilitates the change in attitude needed for criminals to change their behavior. When criminals realize that following the rules is in their best interest, and that they've been their worst enemy, they will be less inclined to break the rules in an attempt to solve their problems.

When speaking of the laws of nations, Montesquieu said, "And if there are others where men are deterred only by cruel punishments, we may be sure that this must, in great measure, rise from the violence of government which has used such penalties for slight transgressions.

It often happens that a legislator, desirous of remedying an abuse, thinks of nothing else; his eyes are open only to this object, and shut to its inconveniences. When the abuse is redressed, you see only the severity of the legislator; yet there remains an evil in the state that has sprung from this severity; the minds of the people are corrupted and become habituated to despotism ..."

The government has a duty in serving the interests of society. The complication is in recognizing the criminal as a part of society, and therefore someone the government has a responsibility towards. Motivating criminals to change into better people is the government's primary responsibility. This is not done merely through punishment. There must be a real effort at rehabilitation.

There are a lot of emotions tied to this issue. The main thing people can't forget is that most prisoners will get out one day. While no politicians, judges, or prosecutors openly say they're opposed to rehabilitation, if their actions and policies create a hostile atmosphere for rehabilitation, they must be condemned for that. If authorities don't have the right attitudes it is impossible for the system to work. That's because their attitude will often impact the criminal's attitude.

The basis for rehabilitation is an accurate perception of reality. This starts with education and a willingness to accept responsibility for one's actions. Without those two pillars, criminals often have an almost childlike view of the world that allows them to believe their failure is a part of some conspiracy to keep them locked up. Authorities unknowingly encourage this view by having negative attitudes and politicizing crime.

Are prisoners just bucking their personal responsibility by rationalizing their failure as a result of a conspiracy? That does play a role, but unless you've been through this insane prison system, you'd never be able to comprehend how people's minds become warped to what's real. What impact would it have on your thinking to have a vicious machine working night and day to make your life miserable? That's what the government is to many prisoners, and there's really no reason for that kind of hostility. If we don't make rehabilitation more than just a feel good phrase in our legal system, a lot more people with a very distorted view of reality will be produced in our prison system.

DESIGNING A LEGAL
JUSTICE SYSTEM

There are certain parameters which are crucial in creating a system that works. A working system must be logical if we want to influence those whom our concept of justice will be practiced upon. How does one understand, much less learn from, a system that has no consistent logical method of applying justice? The patient of our system, the criminal, will reject the organs, rehabilitation, that we'd like to implement in them if we don't make sure that the organs are compatible, that the punishment fits the crime.

One of the reasons that punishments have become so severe, is that anger plays a large part in our public discourse on crime. Anger is not logical. More importantly, it's a strange government that tries to teach criminals not to let anger affect their decision making processes, while allowing anger to be the primary motive for passing all these tough laws and prison sentences.

In prison, criminals are taught that anger causes you to see situations and others as you imagine them, not as they are. That anger creates the illusion that you are doing something about a problem when in reality you're only making it worse. That anger can provide people with a false sense of power and control, overshadowing its potential dangers and consequences. That anger supplies a false sense of superiority, making it difficult to understand situations and people.

The government is making all these same errors in the way they allow anger to influence how they treat criminals. Very often, the Bible is invoked to justify these same policies. Allow me to do the same, "You shall not bear hatred for your brother in your heart. Though you may have to reprove your fellow man, do not incur sin because of him." Leviticus 19:17.

While anger must be eliminated if we are going to make a logical approach to justice, fairness must be the ingredient that takes its place. The concept that justice is blind means that everyone should expect the same treatment under the same circumstances, "You shall not act dishonestly in rendering judgment. Show neither partiality to the weak nor deference to the mighty, but judge your fellow men justly." Leviticus 19:15.

Is that what our current system offers? One punishment that is not given out impartially is the death penalty. There are two reasons for this. The first is that there are political motivations in determining when prosecutors go for the death penalty. Take O.J. Simpson's case as an example. The prosecutors said they would not request the death penalty if Simpson was convicted. If a poor, unknown, black man had been charged with slaughtering two white people with a knife, is there any doubt that the prosecutor would have asked for the death penalty?

The second reason is that money does play a large role in what kind of legal defense you have. "Where there is competent counsel at the trial level, which has been a rare occurrence, the success rate of prosecutors in getting the death penalty, hovers near zero," said Eric M. Freedman, a professor of Constitutional law at Hofstra.

Since the death penalty is popular and gets headlines for judges and prosecutors, it is the most self-serving punishment in our legal political system. That's not to say that in some cases it isn't deserved or appropriately pursued, but in the overall big picture, it's impossible to apply this punishment consistently. That, by itself, makes the death penalty categorically inconsistent with justice.

No system will fix our crime problem since society must make real changes above and beyond just passing new laws. There is a lot wrong with our current system though, which only exacerbates our overall problem. The system we create should be immune from any structural favoritism, while promoting those who can be influenced to better themselves.

In this new system, if a person took any felony charge to a jury trial and was convicted, the jury would decide what the sentence would be. The jury would have three options of what sentence they would give. The majority would rule, and if there was a tie, the judge would be the tie-breaker. The jury would choose between a minimum, a medium and a maximum sentence. This would eliminate much of the rhetoric by judges at sentencing. Here's a chart that shows what the three options could be:

Felony	Minimum	Medium	Maximum
Class A	13 years-life	20 years-life	life-no parole
Class B	10-20	15-30	20-40
Class BC	5-10	7-14	10-20
Class C	3-6	4-8	5-10

| Class D | 1-2 | 2-4 | 3-6 |
| Class E | 1 y. prob. | 2 y. prob. | 1-2 y. prison |

The class A felony carries a life sentence and the years for the minimum and medium dictate how much time must be served before seeing the parole board. Parole boards, as can be seen by Thompson's letter in Rehabilitation, are very politicized. That is why only the worst crime should subject the offender to that process. If a person is deemed a threat to public safety, they will be denied parole. I think there is a benefit in not shutting the door completely in that you give people a reason to have some hope and to have a positive attitude. There will be times when people change, and the situation allows a serious consideration for parole.

The other classes of felonies give you a range between what years a person can get out. What dictates when a person gets out would be what they do in prison. If a person got ten to twenty years, what they did during those first ten years would dictate how much longer they would have to do. For every year the prisoner worked, went to school, took programs, or did volunteer work, they would earn a year back. They could earn up to half their time back. Imagine the change in attitudes of prisoners when they know that if they did what they were supposed to, the state would have to release them early. In the past, prisoners going to school, working, taking programs, behaving, etc…, were things to be considered for determining early release. There was no established standard and too many people were involved in making those determinations. It was impossible to have any consistency. Now we have another extreme in truth in sentencing where nobody gets out early. Goals are a natural part of life, and we should have a system that promotes people to have goals.

"It is an essential element of justice that the role and processes for measuring parole readiness be made known to the inmate. This knowledge can greatly facilitate the earnest inmate toward his own rehabilitation. It is just as important for an inmate to know the rules and basis of the judgment upon which he will be granted or denied parole as it was important for him to know the basis of the charge against him and the evidence upon which he was convicted. One can imagine nothing more cruel, inhuman, and frustrating than serving a prison term without knowledge of what will be measured and the rules determining whether one is ready for release; Justice can never be a product of unreasoned judgment." said Everette M. Porter.

We should also have a system that promotes people to plead guilty, when they are, to avoid the enormous expense of a jury trial and appeals. The current favoritism which dictates who gets the plea bargains must be changed. It degrades the system. To do so, we need another set of guidelines. In Government Waste, I recommended that the prosecutor should bring a deal within two weeks of arrest, and I maintain that. In many cases however, no deals are offered. If someone wants to plead guilty anyway, a standard should exist that offers a minimum of protections while maintaining a degree of consistency. The standard should be that anyone that pleads guilty can get no more than medium punishment that they would have gotten if they'd taken it to a jury trial. If they are a first time offender, they can get no more than the minimum.

Judges would have the option of giving less time than the guidelines stipulate if they feel the punishment is too severe. An example would be if a juvenile did five armed robberies. That's fifty to a hundred years under the minimum at trial. If the judge felt the juvenile had potential to be rehabilitated, he might give him something like twelve to twenty-four years.

The guidelines for the penalties at trial would therefore become a mandatory maximum for those who want to plead guilty. One must understand that if you commit a crime in a little hick town that has no crime, they will sometimes bury you in prison just so a judge or prosecutor can show off. For the same crime in a big city, you might not even get a quarter of the punishment that they'd give in a small town.

Since rehabilitation would be a factor in sentencing in this system, a prisoner would have the opportunity to file for one sentencing modification hearing. After serving five years, a prisoner would become eligible to file a motion explaining why there should be a sentence modification. If the judge feels the prisoner's motion has merit, he may order a hearing.

Once a prisoner is released, the amount of time they'd do on parole would be based on whatever time they had left on their sentence. If they had life however, they'd always be supervised by a parole agent. So, if a person had ten to twenty years, and they were released after twelve, they'd have eight years left to do on parole. Right now, there is way too much time on paper, parole or probation, being given out. The result is that parole agents are overwhelmed by huge case loads and they end up unable to monitor the felons who really need to be monitored.

While it sounds slick for judges to sentence people to all this time on probation and parole, it actually creates a risk to public safety. When felons have ten, fifteen, or twenty years on paper hanging over their head, that means if they make any mistake, they can be revoked for the whole sentence. A fellow who just did a stretch in the penitentiary does not want to return for some minor infraction, like smoking a joint. Yet, because they are not too bright, this is often the situation they put themselves into. These felons have the potential to become extremely dangerous. Why would they go and see their parole officer when they know they're dirty? Why would they allow themselves to be peacefully apprehended when they're facing so much time? What do they have to lose by going on a crime spree once they've already violated the conditions of their parole?

To avoid this danger, two policies could be implemented. The first is that because people are being given so much time on paper, they are bound to fail eventually. Therefore, unless a person is serving a life sentence, or is a sex offender that needs extended monitoring, anyone that serves five years of probation or parole without going back to prison should have the rest of their sentence vacated. This will cut down on case loads and allow parole officers to focus on those who really need to be watched.

The second policy is that rather than have a catch me if you can system, parolees who relapse should have the option of turning themselves in as dirty. I'm not talking about new felonies, just the run of the mill foolishness, like drug and alcohol use. The first time someone turned themselves in, they'd have to take a three month drug and alcohol program. The second time they'd get revoked for a year. The third time would be two years, and so on. As long as they informed their parole officer, before urinalysis, they'd have a safety net. Right now, America's prison population is packed with people in for violating probation or parole. Some do more time on the revocation than they did on the initial sentence. The public has an interest in having a more efficient parole system.

As to the sentencing guidelines, some will think it's too lenient, others that it is too severe. Each state's legislature would have to draw their own conclusions. I looked at current and past sentencing guidelines to make my minimum, medium and maximum sentence chart. I tried to make it as severe as possible, understanding the political climate regarding crime, while maintaining a degree of reasonableness. While those numbers are very important, if they are too severe you eliminate the incentive to plead guilty, the framework of this system is its main attribute. It establishes a tone of fairness and consistency that can give the public, criminals, and those who work in this legal justice system the confidence that justice is actually being served.

Part II

"The peculiar evil of silencing the expression of an opinion is that it is robbing the human race; posterity as well as the existing generation; those who dissent from the opinion, still more than those who hold it. If the opinion is right, they are deprived of the opportunity of exchanging error for truth; if wrong, they lose what is almost as great a benefit, the clearer perception and livelier impression of truth, produced by its collision with error.

It is necessary to consider separately those two hypotheses, each of which has a distinct branch of the argument corresponding to it. We can never be sure that the opinion we are endeavoring to stifle is a false opinion; and if we were sure, stifling it would even be an evil still."

John Stuart Mill

UNDERSTANDING IRAQ

Comprehending the problem in Iraq and figuring out a resolution requires an understanding of history. The problem is that history does not seem to be a strength for either the Bush administration or those who work in America's media. When people are consistently surprised by how events transpire, it's a good indication that they are in over their heads. The lack of foresight by both media and administration shows that either these two groups didn't do their homework, or they consciously made a decision to toe the party line and keep dissent to a minimum. In either case, we have a tragic failure on the part of both institutions that must be corrected, to avoid repeating the mistake. Sadly, the war in Iraq would have never happened had anything been learned from Vietnam.

President Bush is not the first American to allow emotions to dictate foreign policy over logic and reason. In the 1950's, some American elements sympathized and supported the Vietnamese revolutionaries who were rebelling against the French in what was then French Indochina. Their logic was based on the simplistic idea that colonialism was bad and therefore the French were wrong to impose their rule on these people. I'm sure the Native Americans would love it if our government applied this same logic in the United States and gave them all of their land back. To make a long story short, at the eleventh hour, the American government realized that it might not be such a good idea if the Communist guerrillas were to win and so they offered the French air support at the pivotal battle of Dien Bien Phu. With typical Gallic pride, the French refused this offer. This isn't to say that the U.S. hadn't been aiding the French in Vietnam before Dien Bien Phu. On June 29, 1950, America began sending C-47 cargo planes to Vietnam with supplies for the French. Being a democracy however, official support by the government did not automatically translate into support by the whole country. There were a number of critics in the U.S., just as in France, who opposed France's involvement in Vietnam. Much of this opposition stemmed from the U.S. government's initial opposition to the idea of France resuming colonial rule after World War II. The French government viewed these anti-war elements in France and America as the root cause of their failure in Vietnam.

Despite the friction between France and the U.S.A., French President Charles De Gaulle realized that the Americans were in fact an ally and that he shouldn't withhold sound advice from new American President John F. Kennedy, who was then contemplating getting the U.S. involved in Vietnam. In May of 1961, De Gaulle told Kennedy, "I predict to you that you will, step by step, be sucked into a bottomless military and political quagmire."

Now, what would the French know about Vietnam? They'd only been there for three-quarters of a century, which is ironically a lot longer than America would be able to control just the South. President Kennedy wasn't as condescending as Bush and Co. in that he didn't go into a childish rant about freedom fries, and our media wasn't yet enough of a lap dog to go into spin mode insulting the French for not supporting our decision and repeating their mistake. Yet Kennedy did have the arrogance of Bush in that he thought that since America was so much bigger and more powerful than France, that we couldn't learn anything from their experience. Where France failed America would succeed! Then came the evacuation of Saigon, the most humiliating moment in American history.

Most Americans who don't know about these historical facts will find that they are eerily reminiscent of how President Bush handled French President Jacques Chirac's opposition to the invasion of Iraq. Real allies stand up and tell their friends when they are about to make a mistake, regardless of exposure to ridicule. While the French were willing to face the fire, our own politicians did not have the heart to stand up and question Bush in any real detail about his war plan. Again, what would the French know about Iraq? The French, of all the Western countries, have had the most involvement with the Arab world, and they have over five million Arabs living in their country. Much of their experience and knowledge comes from having a colony called Algeria. The French had a war there in the 1950's that was very similar to what is going on now in Iraq.

In Algeria, the French faced the unconventional warfare of the guerrilla, terrorist, which led to the tragedy of French authorities torturing suspects for information. The parallel between what happened in Algeria and what happened at Abu Ghraib and other places in Iraq is disappointing. Had we had an open and thorough debate with France about their reservations for going to war in Iraq, we could have better prepared our soldiers for the obstacles they would soon face. Instead of that approach, our government and media chose to insult France and make childish jokes about their military capabilities. I'm sure all that false bravado is of great consolation to the families of those who died or were maimed in Iraq, only to find that there were no weapons of mass destruction.

When war is on the horizon, politics and human nature have evolved very little over the last 2,000 years. "Beware the leader who bangs the drums of war in order to whip the citizenry into a patriotic fervor, for patriotism is indeed a double edged sword. It both emboldens the blood just as it narrows the mind. And when the drums of war have reached a fever pitch and the blood boils with hate and the mind has closed, the leader will have no need in seizing the rights of the citizenry. Rather, the citizenry, infused with fear and blinded by patriotism, will offer up all of their rights unto the leader and gladly so. How do I know? For this is what I have done. And I am Caesar." That is Julius Caesar, who understood that once you got the populace emotional about an issue, especially war, all reason was cast aside. This is why our government has categorized our crime, cultural and drug problems in war terminology. The reason many people throughout history were skeptical about a democracy working, is based on the premise that the masses are way too easy to manipulate. For the moment, America is proving them correct. In theory, we do have defenses, a free press and an educated populace. In practice, both parties have been inept.

Insulting the French was not enough for President Bush to fuel the fire of war however. He took the additional step of having Colin Powell go to the U.N. and lie to the entire world about Iraq having weapons of mass destruction. Any war you lie to justify is not a good idea. Yet, has the U.S. sent anyone back to the U.N. to apologize to the rest of the world for lying to them? Until that happens, we must assume that this misinformation was deliberate, since anyone with a conscience who had made an error of that magnitude would have been so ashamed that apologizing would be their first step in taking responsibility for their mistake. How disgraceful for America that those foreign leaders that were foolish enough to send troops based on Powell's deception had to explain to their constituents why they trusted the Americans. Leaders in countries like France, Germany and Russia can be thankful that they didn't buy the rhetoric.

It doesn't seem to bother Bush however that as a result of his attempt to mislead the world into war with Iraq, we have lost a lot of credibility on the world stage. The loss of trust in the word of the American Government is something Al Qaeda could have never dreamed to accomplish. America is now impotent in the world of diplomacy and must rely more than ever on the U.N. The problem is we have also undermined the U.N.'s credibility. We used U.N. weapons inspectors before the war, who advised us to give Iraq more time. They were ignored. The real purpose of using weapons inspectors was to present a façade of a legitimate process leading to war.

The contempt Bush and his political allies have for the U.N., makes our new dependence on the U.N. even more ironic. In matters dealing with North Korea and Iran, we must now rely on institutions like NATO and the U.N. to do most of the bargaining because America's word means nothing, thanks to the gaffs of Bush and Co. Think about this, just before invading Iraq, weapons inspectors took their Al Samoud missiles, because they had too long of a range. Why would you invade a country that's willing to let you take whatever forbidden weapons you can find? What country will now allow U.N. weapons inspectors to disarm them, when there is no guaranty that complying will prevent their country from subsequently being invaded?

With Iraq, you have the argument that Saddam Hussein, like colonialism, was bad and needed to be removed. Yet, nobody asked what was going to fill the vacuum? When we realized, too late, that the Communists would be the ones to take power in Vietnam, we compounded our mistake of opposing French colonialism by attempting to intervene in a civil war between North and South Vietnam. A plan? What plan?

In Saddam, it is true they had a tyrant. Yet the only way he could rule Iraq, with three different ethnic groups that hated each other, was to be a tyrant. Furthermore, his tyranny never bothered Americans when he was our ally, fighting against Iran. Once we removed him from power, we had to have a tremendous number of troops to fill that vacuum and keep the peace. We didn't. After the initial shock of the invasion, the Iraqi radicals got comfortable and began slaughtering their fellow countrymen. Despite all the bloodshed, Bush has for years been content to "Stay the course." This begs the question, does Bush in fact see his policy as a success since the result is Muslims killing each other on a level so bad that Iraq might never again rise to become a nation of any importance?

Either Bush is the dumbest President in American history, with an uncanny inability to foresee any of the possible consequences to his decisions, or he likes the results. The rhetoric used to justify invading Iraq, "To fight the terrorists over there, so we don't have to fight them over here," would lead one to believe that privately, Bush is pleased with how things are going in Iraq. How much better could it get for Bush, rather than "Fighting them over there," they end up fighting each other over there? Why would Bush want to put a stop to that? Of course this would mean that Bush sees all Muslims as terrorists. Is that too far fetched? Then what was the link between Saddam Hussein and Al Qaeda, other than that they were both Muslims?

What will become of Iraq? Since we can't allow a tyrant to emerge and restore order, we have to figure out what these three groups, Sunnis, Shiites and Kurds, want. If they would like to split up and create their own independent states, then they need to realize that they'll probably end up being a satellite of one of the neighboring powers with no real power of their own. The Shiites would fall under Iran's sphere of influence and the Sunnis could go with either Syria or more likely with Saudi Arabia. The Kurds have the most likely chance of real independence, but only if the Turks to their north don't feel threatened that this development will give their own Kurdish minority impetus for rebellion. As the violence continues between these factions, the chances of having a united, democratic Iraq diminishes.

Attempting to bring democracy to Iraq reminds me of the old quarrel between the French philosophers Voltaire and Montesquieu. Voltaire believed that his philosophical views on politics were universal in their applicability. Montesquieu felt there was no universally valid solution and that what suited man in one climate might not suit him in another. By climate he meant cultural climate, which was believed to be influenced by geography, temperature and other physical characteristics of the environment that people live in. This ideology was a stepping stone to the modern comprehension of sociology. This debate is at the heart of whether we can bring democracy to a nation such as Iraq. This matter was so serious to philosophers, that Voltaire and his followers did not attend Montesquieu's funeral. Only Diderot attended. Too bad our leaders don't take these issues as seriously as the philosophers, even though the philosophers were dealing with an abstract concept while our politicians are making real decisions that affect people's lives. Yet America's leaders continue to operate in a pre-enlightenment mind set.

One shouldn't be surprised that if our politicians can't learn from Vietnam, which was only a few decades ago, that they wouldn't bother to learn from philosophers who tackled these same questions centuries ago. If we look at America's history, we can conclude that Montesquieu was vindicated. Our concept of democracy has changed over the years according to our cultural development. Perhaps the ideal time in our nation's history to try and convert Islamic countries to democracy would have been during prohibition, since our culture would have been easier for them to accept at that time.

Voltaire however was not all wrong. There are certain basic tenets of democracy that are universal in their scope. Without a free press and elections for example, you can't claim democracy. A democracy is a combination of fluid and rigid elements. We need not start from scratch however in trying to apply democracy to the Muslim world. Turkey is a Muslim democracy, and they should have been the model for Iraq. Not enough was done to solicit Turkish help, another area where our lack of diplomacy has hindered us. From a psychological standpoint, it is much easier for Iraqis to accept the idea of becoming more like Turkey than it is to become like the "Great Satan". At least to the radicals. Using sociology is not such a bad thing.

Had Bush bothered to have a post-invasion plan, he could have kept a united Iraq with three states. Baghdad would have to be the administrative capital from which the three states would share power. Baghdad should have been divided into three zones and each group made to buy or trade land to get it all worked out so that they each had a section. Unpleasant yes, but look at the alternative. Wholesale slaughter and chaos with no possibility of an orderly solution. Some of the capital's population should have been forced out of the city altogether and given land somewhere in their group's zone, just to make Baghdad easier to control.

Each state would get a share of the oil revenue based on population. From that revenue, the states should pay for police, schools, roads and other infrastructure. Realizing that their leaders would determine how their money is spent, would motivate people to participate in elections. Each state would be penalized by a deduction in funds any time one of their members committed a homicide against a member of a different ethnic group. If a Shiite gets murdered by a Sunni, then the Sunni state would lose a hundred thousand dollars of their oil money which would go directly to the victim's family. Once you give the powers in control of each state an incentive to quell the violence, then they'll start enforcing their own laws. Furthermore, since all groups are profiting from the oil, it would deter saboteurs from blowing up pipelines.

The financial incentive is important in that it helps align U.S. goals with those of the people of Iraq. America's goals cannot be realized unless they can persuade the people of Iraq that they have a common interest. Only when the people of Iraq begin working with the U.S. to achieve those goals is any victory possible for either group.

Obviously, there are a lot more details in the three-state one-nation plan. If we do in Iraq what we do in the U.S.A. though, which is tie everything with money, things will start functioning as the wheels get greased. That economic element seems to be applicable universally. President George W. Bush should have been able to figure that out, he did get an M.B.A. from Yale after all.

WAR STRATEGY

Is the Bush administration making the error of attempting to fight the war on terror using Cold War strategies? Military history is full of examples of leaders, both political and military, who wanted to fight the next war with the outdated strategies used to fight the last one. Since two Cold War relics, Rumsfeld and Cheney, were the dominant influences in formulating the war plan in Iraq, this possibility must be considered.

The fight against communism did not start with the Cold War however. To understand why communism eventually fell would require an examination of the bigger historical picture. Just after the Bolsheviks took power in Russia, they made their first act of aggression against a Western nation. Once the expansionist ideology of communism found a nation to take root in, the struggle to keep this weed from spreading began.

In 1920, Russia attempted to forcefully convert Poland into a communist state. The importance of Russia's failure in that attempt was best summarized at the time by Lord D'Abernon, British Ambassador to Berlin: "If Charles Martel had not checked the Saracen conquest at the Battle of Tours, the interpretation of the Koran would now be taught at the schools of Oxford, and her pupils might demonstrate to a circumcised people the sanctity and truth of the revelation of Mahomet. Had Pilsudski and Weygand failed to arrest the triumphant advance of the Soviet Army at the Battle of Warsaw, not only would Christianity have experienced a dangerous reverse, but the very existence of Western civilization would have been imperiled. The Battle of Tours saved our ancestors from the Yoke of the Koran; it is probable that the Battle of Warsaw saved Central, and parts of Western Europe from a more subversive danger—the fanatical tyranny of the Soviet."

The struggle against communism then moved to Germany. Marx and Engels were German Jews that migrated to England. Their intent was for Germany to put their economic theories into practice. They would have never guessed that Russia would be applying their ideology first. After World War I, Germany was economically devastated. Under these circumstances, the Communists grew into a real threat. Who would lead the fight to save Germany from becoming a communist state?

Adolf Hitler's rise in politics was due to his being a staunch anti-communist. Much of his book Mein Kampf is about his views towards Communists and Jews, which he viewed as part of the same evil. Since German business owners didn't want to end up losing their assets under a communist system, where everything would be nationalized, they supported Hitler. This is a perfect example of how fear can override reason in a democratic state.

After rising to power, Hitler's agenda was to consolidate power to a degree sufficient to inevitably take on Russia. One of his first steps was the Anti-Comintern Pact, signed by Germany, Italy and Japan. After the creation of this coalition to fight communism, Mussolini stated, "We are the axis around which the world will spin." This is where the term "Axis" powers came into being. The subsequent invasion of most of Germany's neighboring countries was done as part of a bigger strategy to consolidate European power to take on the Communists in Russia. The Fascists viewed every evil they did as justified, based on the concept that it was all necessary to fight the greater evil of communism.

On the 22nd of June, 1941, Operation Barbarossa began. The Nazis made their bid to destroy communism once and for all. No fighting in world history can compare to the slaughter in the struggle between these two demons. Take all the Americans that have ever died in war, multiply by about twenty, and that's how many men, women and children perished on the Eastern front.

When America entered the war, they were in no hurry to enter the battle of mainland Europe. Russia became the West's beast of burden, through which most of the work of defeating the Nazi's would be done. Eighty-five percent of German casualties came from fighting against Russia. Germany was also serving the West by weakening Russia for after the war. This infuriated Stalin, who repeatedly begged Roosevelt and Churchill to start a second front in Western Europe. However, in the beginning of WWII, Hitler offered Stalin the opportunity of sharing in the robbery of Poland. Having been a bank robber in his youth, Stalin could not resist. The West had not forgotten this treachery, and Russia paid dearly.

Finally, on June 6, 1944, almost five years after WWII started, Normandy was invaded. It was time for the allies to step in and keep the Western half of Europe from eventually falling into the hands of the Communists. Eisenhower allowed the Russians to have the "honor" of taking Berlin. The Battle of Berlin cost the Russians another 100,000 casualties. Two-thirds of German women also paid the price of being raped after the victory in Berlin.

It was then that, as Churchill famously stated, an "Iron Curtain" fell across Eastern Europe. The struggle against communism would then take many forms. Internally, there were a number of people who struggled against Communist rule. Externally, there was a series of wars by proxy. North Korea and North Vietnam were used to fight against the West. Afghanistan was used to fight against Russia. There were also a number of civil wars where America and Russia supported the rebels, or those in power, who were on their side.

In the 1980's leaders like Reagan, Thatcher, and Pope John Paul II, took a more indirect approach to fighting communism. They realized that the battle of ideology was more important than a physical confrontation. Since both super-powers had enough nuclear weapons to wipe out the earth, and still do, it became obvious that cultural and economic pressure, as well as diplomacy, were the means by which the most influence could be exerted.

The ideological war took its biggest step from within the Iron Curtain. The Solidarity Movement in Poland was the first step that eventually led Russians to challenge and examine themselves, their beliefs and their leadership. This period, that preceded the fall of communism, was appropriately named glasnost, "open-ness." Can any false doctrine live when exposed to the light?

Clearly the fight against communism was fought in a number of ways. It is simplistic to claim that any one event or person was responsible for the fall of communism. It was a historical, political movement that was born, grew, with-ered and died in a life span of about eight decades. Every single person, group, nation, religion or political ideology that opposed communism contributed to creating the pressure that caused its implosion. While that external pressure was important, internal defects also played an important role in its doom. Humanity is too ingenious for its own good however. It is that ingenuity that allows people to live under false concepts, systems, or leaders for great periods of time. Just as the fight against communism didn't begin when America entered the struggle after WWII, the fight against militant Islam did not begin on September 11th. Americans need to lose their self-centered, world historical view if they wish to understand and address these global problems.

Unlike the Cold War, we cannot out-spend an enemy that relies on the poppy harvest of Afghanistan as its main source of income, though burning the harvest every year would be a nice start. Sure, we should go after their assets and any sources of income, but that alone won't do it. In fact, we are more likely to break our own bank through reckless war spending. Al Qaeda is not a governmental adversary, and therefore doesn't have the same functions or responsibilities as a traditional national foe. While we can't bankrupt Al Qaeda, we can expose the bankruptcy of their ideology.

Unlike communism, militant Islam is not an ideology that needs a state to exist. Therefore, using another nation as a battlefield to fight a proxy war makes little sense. Iraq was intended to be the central front on the war on terror, but that was naive. We are now in the position of being the beast of burden for Iran, since we eliminated their traditional enemy by destroying the Sunni grip on power in Iraq. When America leaves, Iran will be the scavenger that profits. The only way a proxy war works is when you recruit someone else to do the fighting for you. In the case of Iraq, destabilizing the region is counter-productive since it only creates more recruits and opportunities for terrorists to kill or wound Americans.

Hatred is free, but the consequences are not. We have to be selective in the way we attack our foes, so as not to alienate even more people and feed the rationale for that hatred. This means that we must exercise restraint and use force only when no other options are available. We cannot afford to re-learn all the lessons from the Cold War, just to arrive at the same conclusion; that it's more about winning the war of ideas than any battle with bullets. How do we expose the people of the Middle East to the virtue of our beliefs and vision, when our leadership fails to have either?

EXPORTING CULTURE

The Middle East is a perfect example of why it is important to try and improve the living standards of poorer nations around the world. In the twentieth century we had an opportunity to demand that changes be made in the social and political structures of Middle Eastern nations when Western oil companies were building the infrastructures that would lead to the vast amount of wealth that would eventually be accumulated by tyrants such as Saddam Hussein. We decry the palaces, yachts, and extravagant living of such people, yet we are the ones that enabled these tyrants to obtain such unnaturally powerful and undemocratic positions over their people.

When all the oil wells and pipelines were being put in, Western oil companies and their governments thought of nothing but the money they'd soon make. They didn't demand social or political concessions, because another Western oil company would have come in and taken their business, by not making those same types of demands. It was the responsibility of politicians of those governments, with oil companies doing business in the Middle East, to identify their long term interests and form a united front. Not one drop of oil would have been pumped out of the ground without Western technology, but that leverage was thrown away by Western politicians too dumb to see this opportunity. Rather than demanding freedoms for the people in these countries, the West turned a blind eye towards despotism. Tyrants, being true to their nature, then pointed at us as the villains behind all the suffering of the Arab people, despite the fact that we were the ones responsible for making people like Saddam Hussein and Osama Bin Laden rich beyond measure. Good old Western technology is the backbone behind all Middle Eastern wealth.

It seems that Western nations have not been able to figure out that giving away technology is very dangerous and often leads to resentment more than appreciation. Looking at our own history, as the West developed scientifically, it also developed culturally, so that the technology served our social structure. At times, there have been bumps in the road. World War I & II were two that had the potential to destroy Western civilization. To separate technology and culture is a dangerous game and we jeopardize our future when we give technology to nations that are not socially prepared. China has the potential to become a much bigger problem than the Middle East, if we don't start attaching strings to giving them the benefits of Western technology. Greed for oil caused us to overlook tyranny in the Middle East and greed for cheap products allows us to overlook tyranny in China.

Even societies that have a developed Western culture can be undermined by political instability to turn good technology into a deadly tool. Hitler's Germany is a perfect example. The National Socialists, Nazis, took two thousand years of European history and culture, and burned it in great bonfires. The Nazis castrated Germany culturally, and then created a fraudulent culture, elitism through race, rather than achievement. As a result, allied bombs turned German cities into bonfires where a lot more than books were burnt. This was despite the fact that Germany had some of the best scientific minds in the world. At the beginning of World War II, the German army was technologically superior to any on earth. Yet, without the correct social infrastructure and political leadership, Germany ended up destroying itself. This should be a lesson to Americans who pride themselves on being at the cutting edge of technology, and of having such a potent military. It is not enough by itself to guaranty prosperity, and these blessings are not given to lord it over weaker nations.

In many parts of the Third World, we turn a blind eye towards tyranny so that we can get cheap products. Obviously, most of these nations won't become a threat to the U.S., but look at North Korea. Just a little piece of land on the globe, but due to advanced technology, without corresponding political and social development, a serious threat emerges. Is it too late to reverse the mistakes made by Western leaders since World War II?

One of the reasons Western nations have ignored tyranny, though it's no excuse, is the Cold War. We were so focused on fighting the evils of communism that we overlooked a lot of other evils, especially those of our own. The fall of communism is a fairly recent historical development, but in the modern age, great leaps occur in short stretches. It is now time for us to take advantage of the fall of communism, show the world our vision, and help Third World nations realize the benefits of our cultural, political and technological development. The three must go together or not at all. By failing to do so, we are actually forfeiting our victory in the Cold War and creating opportunities for other problems to manifest themselves in the Third World.

A lot of people complain about Hugo Chavez, but really, we deserve Hugo Chavez. While I disagree with communism, Chavez is reminding us that there's a lot of work to be done in the Third World. While ill formulated, I think Chavez at heart simply wants to bring a higher standard of living for his people and we, who profit greatly from the labor and resources of countries like Venezuela, have not offered much leadership in creating that. Until we do, there will probably be more leaders like Chavez to deal with, in the future.

A lot of status quo journalists and politicians will oppose the idea of doing anything to solve problems in the Third World, because we have enough problems that need solving here. If only we were addressing the problems "here", I'd be more than happy to entertain that argument. However, since we've played a role in the creation of the social, political and economic structures of many Third World countries, it would be irresponsible to wash our hands "à la Pilate" of the fate these nations face. Yet, that is exactly what might happen in Iraq in the near future. There is a correlation between what goes on in the Third World and what goes on in the developed nations. Solving problems "there" goes a long way towards solving problems "here."

Often times, conservative politicians frame their domestic cultural agenda in moral terms. Is their morality limited to our borders? Should not the same moral principles be adhered to in our foreign policy? If conservatives can argue that Western culture should maintain a role in determining what kind of laws we have here, should not that same Western culture impact our relationship with foreign nations? Should not labor standards, freedom of speech and religion, amongst other Western rights, be a prerequisite to trade with these developing nations? Shouldn't we be a positive influence and show them the way? Or do we simply serve Mammon? If Western culture stops growing simply so that some businessmen can pilfer the poor, then Western Culture is dead.

Where does the moral standing come for the government to condemn drug dealers, who are also in it for the almighty dollar, when the government allows big businesses to do pretty much anything overseas as long as it makes money? We condemn the drug dealer because the negative consequences of their business is so obvious and immediate. Yet, big businesses often engage in practices that while in the short term don't appear bad, in the long term they can undermine the stability of an entire region. Nowhere is this more true than in the Middle East, where oil companies have enriched tyrants. We should not limit our moral view to how our businesses support tyrants that oppose us, it is just as evil when we financially support villains who, while our allies, are brutal on their people.

One of the main purposes of modern conservatism is to make sure we don't lose sight of our culture in the midst of all the spectacular technological developments domestically, while at the same time making sure we promote our culture hand in hand with the technology we export internationally. It is a valuable role that must be taken seriously by true modern conservatives. That is not what is happening.

On the domestic front, conservatives have thrown their weight into so called culture wars without realizing that the stakes are much higher in the international playing field. While domestically conservatives worry about whether homosexuals should get married, China's one child policy has led parents to choose over-whelmingly to have one male child. With such an unbalanced ratio of males to females, China will either have a lot of homosexuals, or females will be allowed to have multiple husbands, or prostitution will skyrocket. My guess is that with so many males and so few females, China will become militant and expansionist. Faced with this social dilemma, it becomes difficult to promote our culture in an environment that is like something out of a science fiction novel. Yet, while big businesses that back pseudo-conservatives, continue to make big money off our trade with China, conservatives continue to pound the moral gavel at home to get votes on issues like gay marriage.

While much rhetoric has been made by conservatives about culture wars, notice how little American culture has improved since President Ronald Reagan took office. Since then, conservatives have held their fair share of power, yet how much have they been able to change the culture? Conservatives will complain that their failure is a result of the liberals' control of the media and so on. The problem is that very few conservatives have any understanding of our domestic culture, or how to influence it. In many instances, the same people railing about culture wars are the people with no culture whatsoever. This ignorance is what cripples America as an entity that can export culture to the Third World. Sadly, despite America's economic and technological might, the Europeans might be more fit in leading the charge in exporting Western culture to the Third World. That's a national tragedy which should make any American that loves their country, sick.

Conservatism does have a crucial role, but I don't see any self-proclaimed conservatives in leadership that are true to the calling. We can change that however, and it begins with politicians not serving as the lap dogs of short-sighted big businesses. The conservatives need to understand that all these domestic squabbles, while appearing significant around election time, will mean nothing if we fail to win the culture war on an international level. Liberals must also place a greater emphasis on promoting Western culture internationally. The question is, will politicians be able to see the connection between our future and what's going on in the rest of the world? Foreign policy is irrelevant without a certain degree of diplomacy. The Presidency of George W. Bush has probably been the worst period in the history of the United States in terms of our focus on diplomacy. Arrogantly, Bush tried to use our military to force change in other countries. Exporting culture is not simple, and simple minded leaders will not be up to the task.

LABOR PAINS

In April 2006, there were a large number of demonstrations across the United States by immigrants opposing a proposed immigration law. At the same time there were a large number of demonstrations across France, by young people who opposed a law passed that undermined the legal protections for workers under the age of twenty-six. At the core of both protests was the issue of living standards and what role the government can play to ensure the future economic prosperity of both respective nations.

Most media in the United States were very critical of the young French demonstrators. The general view was that due to such a high youth unemployment rate, the French government was correct to pass legislation that allowed young workers to be fired for any reason during the first two years of employment. This eliminated the costly process of appeals and workers' compensation that the laws currently require. This law would therefore lead to businesses hiring more young workers and help alleviate the high unemployment rate, which had been a major stimulus to the riots that occurred in 2005. The rioting was the work of immigrants, and their children born in France, who felt they were not being given enough job opportunities.

At first glance, it would appear that the American media was correct in its criticism, and that the young French protesters were being unreasonable. Yet, French president Jacques Chirac acquiesced the protesters by canceling the law and promising that the government would utilize other means, financial incentives, to encourage businesses to employ more youth. Sacré Bleu! According to the American business model, the workers can't have it all, and Chirac should have made a stand, or at least that would be the conventional thinking. Is the American business model one to be emulated though?

Upon closer inspection, it appears that the French youth are on to something. While the proposed law would have affected a minority of workers, it undercut the tradition of French working class values. Mock those values if you will, but they are one of the cornerstones of the French Revolution. Their government's reason to exist is based on the idea that its purpose is to serve the working class majority, not the rich land and business owners. The French have all those protections and benefits for their workers mandated by law because they believe that the purpose of work is to enable the worker to enjoy life. The idea of a working poor is an anomaly and if a higher unemployment rate is the price to pay, then the French attitude is, so be it. In a prosperous nation, the goal is not simply working to survive, but rather to continuously raise the standard of living. The French recognized that driving the standard of living down for the sake of some dead end jobs was not only unacceptable, but undemocratic.

How does this bode for France's economic future? By guarantying a strong middle class for years to come, French businesses will continue to have a strong domestic demand for their goods. It would be hard for French car manufacturers such as Peugeot or Renault to survive, if French workers could no longer afford their products. Of course there will be challenges in the global economy for France to face, but they will not be alone. Will workers at General Motors or Ford be able to afford their own company's cars when they finish restructuring? What about the rest of Americans who are losing jobs in manufacturing, and going to lower paying service industry jobs?

In the last French Presidential election, Nicolas Sarkozy won on a platform that promised to chip away at workers' rights and benefits to stimulate job growth. However, Sarkozy is finding out that it's easier to make promises in an election than to deliver the goods. When he tried to enact these reforms, French laborers went on strikes that almost shut down France. Like it or not, unions work.

While it's true that economic growth has been greater for the U.S. than France, that growth has been reflected in the increased wealth of those who own stocks in companies that are profiteering from cutting labor costs. Time and time again, the stocks of companies who announce the layoffs of thousands of U.S. workers have increased in value immediately. While companies claim they'll save millions of dollars as a result of these job cuts, it appears as though the future is being mortgaged for the sake of profits today. For those American workers who have lost their jobs, a more "stagnant" economy like that of France doesn't seem like such a bad deal.

This brings us back to the issue of immigrants in the U.S., and their recent protests against immigration laws. American businesses profit from immigrants who come to America and work for less pay than the average American worker is willing to accept. With a greater labor pool, the value of the unskilled worker decreases and this fosters resentment towards immigrants whose competition allows businesses to pay at a lower scale and drive down the standard of living for unskilled American workers. This resentment is misplaced and the immigration bill that provoked the protests will not change the factors that create the current labor dilemma. While these sort of backlash immigration laws appeal to the emotions and prejudices of their constituents, politicians need to develop a more holistic approach to dealing with labor problems in the global economy.

The primary reason foreigners immigrate to the U.S., is so that they can raise their standard of living. If we wish to encourage people to stay in their own countries, we need to take an interest in increasing the standard of living in those countries. A fence, or criminalizing immigrants, does not address the fundamental issue or thereby solve the problem. Addressing the problem will require Western nations to face some inconvenient truths about their past failures and spend a little money. The good news is that in the long run, Europe and America will profit from that. The bad news is that politicians operate in the short term and are more interested in simple arguments that can appeal to the common, uneducated voter.

The failure of developed nations in the Third World is not a new one. It is an age old economic quandary that we seem to repeat over and over. How do the rich and powerful deal with the weak and poor? In the historical sense, only a short time ago did we finally figure out that it was wrong to enslave our fellow man. Yet, are we any better if we take advantage of him instead of enslaving him? When we see our fellow man struggling to rise out of poverty, and we use him as a laborer to enrich ourselves, while we give him just enough to barely survive, are we morally superior to the slave master? If modernity consists of simply changing the name of slave to sweat shop worker, then we are deceiving ourselves in thinking any progress has been made.

We, in developed nations like our fruit, coffee and clothes cheap. Our businesses have gone into Third World countries to use their people, so that they can make as much money as possible, and provide us with enough goods to satisfy our gluttonous appetites. So far so good, but now we have a problem. Our businesses have figured out that they can also have these people produce the manufactured goods for cheaper than we can. In a truly free market, the developed nations' unskilled workers cannot compete with those of the Third World. This is not a new economic problem but there is a new twist.

In a pure free market, those who own the land and businesses are king, and those who will do the work for the cheapest, get the jobs. This is why we had all those riots around the turn of the twentieth century, and why we developed unions and labor laws. The new twist is that because we have a global market, the workers' plight is not determined on a national scale. Therefore it's not sufficient to get laws passed, either in France to undermine the protections of workers or in the U.S., to cut immigration, that merely address local conditions. Thus the term, "Global Economy".

It is time now that we, in the developed nations, take an interest in our fellow workers in the Third World. The first thing we can do, is pressure our businesses and politicians to make Third World countries pass minimum wage and other labor laws. Obviously, those minimum wages wouldn't start out the same as those in developed nations, but the World Trade Organization, WTO, needs to determine what each of those nations economies can handle. Trade sanctions could be threatened, if they fail to enact those laws.

The WTO was founded in 1994, to enforce the General Agreement on Tariffs and Trade, called GATT. GATT provides protections for patents, trademarks and copyrights. While that is important, it shows that GATT leans heavily towards protecting the rights and interests of those in the developed world. Expanding GATT to include a greater focus on protecting laborers and the environment would show a greater balance towards protecting the rights of those in the developing world. Not everyone is blessed with living in a democratic society, where people can hold the authorities accountable. Using the WTO to lean on those authorities, is the next step in this young organization's maturation.

In developed nations, we have one flat minimum wage, but for the developing world, there could be two or three, depending on the country. Agrarian, service, and manufacturing jobs could each have their own scale. Labor in those countries should gradually increase earnings until they make a similar percentage as laborers in developed nations earn off their companies' profits. For those working in the developed world, what percentage of the profit should go to the laborers is a question worth revisiting. Each sector is different in make-up, but right now, CEOs are earning a ridiculous percentage of the income that companies make.

Generally, you can break down three groups that must share the profit. First you have the owners or stockholders. Then you have the management or white collared workers. Last but hopefully not least is the blue collar laborer. It is the blue collar workers in both poor and rich countries that are getting the short end of the stick. They can remain divided or they can stand together and demand their fair share. A global economy cannot work until we get a global standard of what is fair. Once these standards are implemented, there will no longer be a need for laborers to undercut each other, thereby driving the standard of living down for all workers.

There are businessmen who will be furious about the idea that labor laws should not be confined to the developed world. That to bridge the gap between us and the underdeveloped world, we must require those countries to adopt the standards that have worked so well for us, and are the backbone of our prosperity. Businesses that use cheap labor at .50¢ a day, should get involved in the process, and recognize their malfeasance. Perhaps they won't lose as much of their profits. The cost of some things will go up to pay for this raise, but since those people will now be able to afford to buy our products, our exports will grow. The survival of all unskilled workers in developed nations depends on this. The U.S. is especially vulnerable to this problem due to the high number of high school drop-outs in every major city's public school system. It's not just a moral issue anymore. It's not just a matter a having sympathy for these people. The question is, what kind of world are we going to live in, and leave to future generations.

It all comes back to living standards. If we don't promote their prosperity, their standard of living will eventually impact us. We have been part of the problem by ignoring the taking advantage of laborers in the Third World. Did you think there would be no consequences for this? Is it really worth treating these workers unfairly so that we can get coffee for .25¢ cheaper and a couple extra cents per share on our dividends?

If so, then we deserve what we have coming. Our standard of living continuously eroding, year after year, or haven't you noticed the trend? There is absolutely no excuse for any country in the 21st century not to have a livable minimum wage and other labor protections. If those of us in developed nations don't promote this, then we have no moral standing. If you believe that a rising tide lifts all ships, then taking an interest in the living standards of those in the Third World will eventually lead to economic benefits for those of us in developed nations. If you want to promote democracy around the world, then realize that the backbone of democracy is a healthy working class. The alternative is the eventual destruction of our own working class, and a return to oligarchy. Or are we already there?

WELFARE REFORM

The Republican Party has taken a lot of credit for reducing the welfare rolls in recent years. Former Governor Tommy Thompson is praised as the one who started it all with his Welfare to Work program, which some other states copied. Should we be skeptical when our great leaders tell us they've solved a problem?

Over the years, since Welfare to Work has been passed, there has been an increase in the number of children who suffer from mental illness in areas where lots of people have been taken off welfare. What's happened is parents who no longer get welfare checks tell their children to go to school and "act crazy" until they get sent to the school psychologist. Once there, the psychologist usually makes a recommendation to see a psychiatrist who then makes a diagnosis that the child is suffering from some kind of mental illness. This results in the parents becoming eligible to collect SSI checks to help take care of their now mentally ill child. This is done with children as young as five years old. I know this because certain criminal elements have informed me of this so called "hustle." While it is amazing what people will do to get around doing some work, it would be helpful if these types of issues weren't so politically charged. People's welfare is at stake, no pun intended, and the focus should be on the children rather than on their parents. It is by focusing on the parents that welfare has become a dirty word, but now look what they are doing to their own children to keep the money coming in.

This scam has also had a devastating impact on public schools in places like Milwaukee. Teachers are so busy trying to deal with disruptive students, that they have less and less time to teach. How will these children get prepared to compete in the global economy? The Republican solution is to allow the good students to go to private schools with their School Choice program, another initiative Wisconsin politicians love bragging about being first on. I'm fine with the choice program, as long as those private schools are required to take the same percentage of students that are eligible for SSI as exists in Milwaukee Public Schools. Everyone loves to berate MPS for what a lousy job they're doing teaching the children, but I suspect that if you gave the private schools these same students who are told by their parents to "act crazy", you'd see a quick decline in the learning environment of the private schools, again through no fault of the teachers.

Another factor for teachers trying to deal with these students is that when they discipline the children, or tell a parent that their child did something wrong, they have to deal with parents who are in fact the root of the problem. The result is that some parents are overly defensive, often making excuses for their child's behavior. Sometimes there are situations where parents become very aggressive and hostile. This can range from parents getting loud and disrespectful, to physical attacks on teachers.

The sad fact is that if you give people incentives to have problems, they'll have problems. The Republicans shouldn't claim to have solved the welfare problem simply by shifting the burden onto Social Security, which has become a different form of welfare with less negative connotations. Then add the fact that these children will one day become adults, collecting SSI for themselves and probably having their children do the same thing. "Hey Doc, what can I say, it runs in the family." This shell game of transferring welfare to SSI will have a devastating impact on Social Security in the long run, which as a result of the baby boom generation becoming eligible for benefits, is already facing a crisis.

Now, think of these children who had nothing wrong with them, other than having bad parents, being doped on medications that we don't have any idea what the long term side effects are. Seeing the stacks of medications that are regularly brought into the cell halls of every prison I've ever been in, I worry about their future. The volume of medications consumed in our prison systems is staggering, and obviously they don't keep people out of prison. I'm not going to go all out and attack psychiatrists, but any drug can be abused, even legal ones. In the system we have set up, it is far too easy to attempt to solve someone's problems through medications. When it comes to medicating children, we need to make that our last possible option.

It doesn't stop there though. Part of the Welfare to Work program requires recipients to go to school to receive their checks. While this has worked well for some, there are people who once again take advantage of the system. These "students" only show up when absolutely necessary to get their checks. They are completely unmotivated and even pretend to be dumber than they are, so they can take more courses and stay longer in school. I understand how if you haven't been in school for ten years you would need to take some remedial courses, but for those who just graduated from High School? How many years of schooling will taxpayers provide while paying these people? All this just so a politician can say people are no longer on welfare! That they are now earning their checks!

Wonderful. We can afford to send people to school who don't want to go, but there are children who want to go to college but can't, because they can't afford it.

There is an old saying, "Statistics lie and liars use statistics." The problem is that in the TV age, where thirty seconds is the average amount of time given to a topic, this saying is even more true. It's easier for politicians to say that everything is working because the number of people on welfare has declined, than it would be for someone to point out exactly what the ramifications of that decline are. I grant that whatever system you have, there will be abuses by people who have no initiative and are basically parasites. At the same time, you have people who are genuinely making an effort to get on their feet and need help. How do we, as a society, find a balance between helping the one, while not allowing the other to bankrupt the system, so that we come to the point where our government doesn't have the resources to deal with the ever increasing number of problems we face. Welfare to Work needs a lot more work before politicians can claim it as a success. Hopefully, rather than defending their pet programs, they'll be willing to recognize that there is always room for improvement.

THE BIBLE AND SCIENCE

The Bible is a collection of books that Jews and Christians believe to be the Word of God. The Jewish Bible, what Christians call the Old Testament, is where we find the story of creation. People who take this story literally, feel that when schools teach the Big Bang or Evolution theory in science class, they are undermining their religion. Some would like a theory of "Creationism" to be taught in science class along with the other theories.

Should there be a controversy? For those Christians who would rather go into a convulsion than believe that the Bible should not always be taken literally, I will quote a passage in the Bible that goes straight to the heart of the issue. "But do not ignore this one fact, beloved, that with the Lord one day is like a thousand years and a thousand years like a day." 2 Peter 3:8. Not only does the Bible use metaphors, but when matters of time are being discussed we must realize that God, an Eternal Being, has a different perspective on time than us human beings.

What is a day? A day is twenty-four hours because that's how long it takes the Earth to make a rotation on its axis. If you go to a different planet, a day is longer or shorter, depending on its speed of rotation. So where was God on the first day? He wasn't on Earth, since on the first day, He created light and the Earth wasn't made yet. Since we must assume that both God and the Bible are logical, this rules out the possibility of a twenty-four hour Earth day from the story of creation.

Let's examine why the word "day" would be used to break up time sequences in the story of creation. Day is used as a metaphor because that's something everyone can understand. Imagine God explaining to the Israelites thousands of years ago how he created the universe in scientific terms. Would they have been able to comprehend it? Today, can we honestly say we comprehend what a million years is, or a billion years? The purpose of the creation story is to make humanity aware that God created everything, including us. He then, for better or worse, gave us dominion over everything.

Amazingly, if we look at the sequence of the story of creation written so long ago, we find that modern science verifies these events. The Big Bang could have just as easily been called the Big Flash. Perhaps scientists felt the Big Flash would be too comical for school kids, and to keep their young minds away from perversion, felt the Big Bang was a safer title. The fact that the Bible focuses on the creation of light first, is actually more logical. The light created is something permanent that we can still see in the sun and stars. Nobody ever heard the bang.

As to evolution, it shows that man didn't come about until fairly recently, compared to sharks and crocodiles. The creation story says man was the last thing God created. We should be rejoicing that science has verified this! As to the whole ape thing, evolution does have what's called a missing link. I take that as being the time God stepped in and created man, thus the inability of science to explain it. What's the problem?

Science is what we can prove through testing and observing the natural world. Faith is the belief of something that can't be proven. If we could prove it, we'd no longer need faith. When Christians falsely create controversies to pretend they are fighting some culture war, it undermines the credibility of the truly faithful. Scientists, many of whom are Christians, are not conspiring to destroy religion. Children learning about science is not going to bring about the destruction of our society. Sex, drugs and violence are everywhere, and students are dropping out of school in huge numbers, yet religious leaders are worried about how science class is being taught? That's the best way of using their time?

The story of creation is very important. It tells us that we were created by an all powerful and ever living God. That despite the madness, there is a plan to all of this, and that we have divine origins. Knowing this should uplift us and motivate us to pursue the greatness of our Maker. When we create something beneficial, we follow in the footsteps of our Creator who looked over His creation and "saw how good it was". Genesis 1:25. We must make sure that when we use our God given abilities to create, we do so for good.

In the Bible's creation story, when God gave man dominion over the Earth, man was not at that point very dominant. Man's dominance was a process that manifested itself over the ages. If a man came across a tiger back in the days, the odds were in favor of the tiger. Today, man foolishly hunts the tiger to the verge of extinction. When you compare man's situation today to that of his past, it is clear that God gave us the intelligence to tame the environment. Science is man using his God given ability to understand and conquer nature. We still have a couple of things to figure out, like how to stop a hurricane, or global warming, but through science we are making the story of creation truer every day. Let the science teachers continue to teach science, and let those who teach religion understand that no scientific fact contradicts religion, if you truly understand religion and science.

For those who would like to continue arguing this controversy, in the hope of proving their religious devotion, consider what Erasmus said regarding the debate over religious matters, and when they will be resolved:

"May not a man be a Christian who cannot explain how the nativity of the Son differs from the the procession of the Holy Spirit? If I believe in the Trinity in Unity, I want no arguments. If I do not believe, I shall not be convinced by reason. The sum of religion is peace, which can only be when definitions are as few as possible and opinion is left free on many subjects. Our present problems are said to be waiting for the next Ecumenical Council. Better let them wait till we see God face to face."

WHO IS REALLY LEFT BEHIND

The Left Behind series of books by Tim LaHaye and Jerry Jenkins have been very popular amongst evangelical and fundamentalist Christians. They have now added a video game, Left Behind-Eternal Forces, to promote their message. This video game has received a lot of criticism for its graphic violence.

While the violence shows their willingness to do anything in the name of Jesus, to make a buck, I was much more intrigued by the fact that they chose Manhattan as the setting for the fight against Antichrist. Is this not what Osama Bin Ladin thought, when he orchestrated the September 11th attacks? Why is Manhattan considered by every fool and crank to be the opening of the abyss?

There is probably more talent in Manhattan, per square mile, than anywhere on earth. As a writer, I would love to live in Manhattan. Working with the best could only enhance my skills. To a writer without much talent, Manhattan might seem to be a scary place. You might get exposed as a hack. Is that why LaHaye and Jenkins hate Manhattan?

Are there bad people in Manhattan? Maybe even a few devils? Just like everywhere else in the world, Manhattan has its share of villains. There are also some very decent people in Manhattan, many of whom are even Christians. Shocking, isn't it?!

Moral superiority, just like racial superiority, requires its practitioners to look down on large groups of people whom they know nothing about. The bigotry of this game allows characters to say, "Praise the Lord," while killing people. This reminds me of the September 11th hijackers who also probably said,"Allah Akbar," as they crashed planes into buildings. Simple good taste should have prevented this game from ever being made.

How could two so-called "Christian" writers be so blind? Apparently, they have not been "saved" from the lure of money. I'm sure both the Taliban and Al Qaeda love this game though, so they can take some consolation in that. This game is not surprising, if you consider the theme of their books. As a Christian, I oppose any work that uses the Book of Revelations for entertainment. This includes the Left Behind books, the TV series "Tribulation" and the movie "End Days" with Arnold Shwarzenegger. The Book of Revelations expressly states, "I warn everyone who hears the prophetic words in this book: if anyone adds to them, God will add to him the plagues described in this book," Rev. 22:18.

When people use the Book of Revelations as a basis for a fictional book or movie script, they are adding their own interpretation of the prophecy. It seems that all the popular media use a similar general formula in their packaging of Revelations, into an entertainment event. Usually they present the seven seals, seven trumpets, seven plagues, and seven bowls as events yet to come. However, there is no way to prove the validity of this interpretation.

One possible interpretation is that since there is no set time period between say the breaking of each seal, these events could take place over a period of decades, if not centuries. Who is to say that some of the seals have not already been broken open and manifested by such historical events as the rise of communism, World War I, the rise of fascism in the 1930's, World War II, the Cold War, which was pretty hot in Korea, Vietnam, Latin America and Africa. In more recent history, the tragedy of Chernobyl, the devastation of Aids, September 11th and the following wars on terrorism. For those who have experienced the horrors of the real world, or know the recent history of man, these events seem just as likely a fulfillment of the prophesies of Revelations as anything that could be created by authors of fiction.

The interpretation that there could be a lengthy time period between these events is supported by what happens after the fifth seal is opened. "They cried out in a loud voice, 'How long will it be, holy and true master, before you sit in judgment and avenge your blood on the inhabitants of the earth?' Each of them was given a white robe, and they were told to be patient a little while longer until the number was filled of their fellow servants and brothers who were going to be killed as they had been," Rev. 6:10-11. Keep in mind, this is after the Four Horsemen of the Apocalypse have been unleashed upon the Earth.

"But of that day and hour no one knows, neither the angels of heaven, nor the Son, but the Father alone." Matt. 24:36.

The deception these Revelations as entertainment works promote, is that people will be able to see events unfold. As a result, many will falsely conclude that they can safely continue in their ways until they see these prophesies begin to be fulfilled. Christ was very clear that He would come as a thief in the night however.

The accepted mark of the beast interpretation is another deception that could be used to make people think they'll know when the end is near, and fool them.

How do we know that the mark is visible to humans or that you'll even know when you've accepted it? "No one could buy or sell except one who had the stamped image of the beast's name or number that stood for its name." Rev. 13:17.

That seems to mean that it will be visible, but remember the temptation of Christ. "Then he took him up and showed Him all the kingdoms of the world in an instant. The devil said to Him, 'I shall give to you all this power and their glory; for it has been handed over to me, and I may give it to whomever I wish,'" Luke 4: 5-6.

That's right, the devil has ruled the world for some time now. Do we see him running around with tail and pitchfork? Of course not. If he decided to mark all his own and test the rest like Job, would we know it? Job didn't, and God liked Job. Could the devil punish those who follow God by driving them out of business and into bankruptcy so they couldn't buy or sell anything? Quite easily, and even more so, after the bankruptcy legislation passed by Bush and the Republican Congress.

The Bible, especially Revelations, is full of metaphors. Perhaps the devil will invisibly mark his own and he'll stamp those on the head who have been indoctrinated into believing in falsehood, while those who do the work of the beast will get a stamp on the hand. So when one writes books misinterpreting prophesy to mislead people, one could earn a stamp on the head and hand and never know it.

I am not foolish enough to claim that I know how to interpret Revelations. I'm only giving you possible alternative interpretations to show you that there are other possibilities besides what LaHaye and Jenkins have written. The Bible is clear on this topic. "Know this first of all, that there is no prophesy of Scripture that is a matter of personal interpretation, for no prophesy came through human will; but rather human beings moved by the Holy Spirit spoke under the influence of God." 2 Peter 1: 20-21.

What this means is that you'll find out what the book of Revelations really means when it's all over. In the meantime, don't let anyone try and interpret for you what it means. Anyone that does, or helps promote someone that does, is a false prophet, of which there will be many. So, "Be watchful! Be alert! You do not know when the time will come," Mark 13:33.

EMERGENCY MEDICAL CARE FUND

The high cost of health insurance is hurting state and federal budgets, as well as American businesses that provide health insurance coverage for their employees. For those in public service, it has always been taken for granted that in exchange for giving up an opportunity of more pay in the private sector, they would get job security and good health coverage working for the government. In Wisconsin, the high cost of health insurance became political when animosity was stirred up against teachers for having what was termed "Cadillac" health insurance coverage. The teachers had this better coverage because in past labor negotiations, they had accepted better health care plans in lieu of pay raises. The jealousy was perhaps rooted in the fact that other state employees, who were in the process of negotiating new contracts, were being asked by the state to make co-payments to maintain their health insurance coverage.

In the private sector, the high cost of health insurance is choking employers' profit margins and cutting into their ability to add new employees. American industries are at a competitive disadvantage against foreign corporations who pay much less for health insurance since most of their employees' health care is provided by their government or not at all. To put the cost of health care for American businesses in perspective, think of the fact that American auto companies spend more in health coverage than they do for steel in the production of each car. Other companies in danger of going bankrupt as a result of the high costs of health insurance, are contemplating cutting their costs by defaulting on their pensions. Without Americans dealing with the high cost of health insurance, they can continue to expect their standard of living to be driven down.

The health insurance industry is not all to blame for this mess. They are a business that functions like any other, to provide a service and make a profit. The health insurance industry can only provide that service at a reasonable cost if the system regarding how health care is paid for, is fair. The law however is set up to make those that are insured cover the costs of the care for the uninsured, which substantially drives up the cost of health insurance. It's a back-door method of having nationalized health care with the health insurance industry being forced to act as the broker.

Here's how it works. By law, no hospital in these United States of America can turn down anyone seeking emergency medical care, which is the most expensive form of care that hospitals provide. To recoup the costs of emergency care provided to the uninsured, the medical bills of the insured are inflated. Those inflated bills then cause health insurance companies to charge more for their coverage.

Some hospitals have moved away from the urban setting because emergency costs are killing their profits. Central cities are seeing less emergency care available for those most in need. Since we don't have national health care, this is not their fault. Hospitals are part of the market economy, and therefore must go where the money takes them.

I believe that as a civilized society, we must continue to require our hospitals to provide emergency medical care to the uninsured. However, if we leave it at that, we are creating an unfunded mandate which someone will have to pay for. That someone is taxpayers and businesses through higher insurance premiums for workers in the public and private sectors. This way of indirectly paying for the health care of the uninsured is more expensive than a direct payment since the broker, the insurance industry, gets a cut.

There are currently almost fifty million people in the United States without health insurance. If people get into an accident, get shot, or have some other misfortune, they could lose all their assets and have their wages garnished until they pay back the hundreds of thousands of dollars they could end up owing from a stay in the emergency room. However, because many of the working uninsured are poor to begin with, the amount they end up paying is a pittance compared to the total cost of their medical bills. This doesn't make it any less of a hardship for the working poor who must make do with even less money from their garnished paychecks, if they are still physically able to continue working.

There is a solution for everyone. If each state would create an Emergency Medical Care Fund and reimburse the hospitals for any emergency care that they provide to the uninsured, it could dramatically cut the cost of health insurance. In order to fund this, every worker that does not have health insurance must pay twenty-five dollars every two weeks, when they get their paycheck, into the fund. The result would be that if anyone without insurance goes to the hospital for an emergency, they will not owe any hospital bills. No garnishment of wages or seizure of property. We require everyone that drives a car to have some form of auto insurance and the principles are no different here. Everyone that works contributes.

Twenty-five dollars multiplied by twenty-six paychecks a year is only $650, slightly over the average monthly cost of a regular health insurance policy these days. That's a good deal even if it only covers emergencies. For every ten million uninsured workers, state governments would now collect 6.5 billion dollars per year to reimburse hospitals for treating the uninsured for emergencies. While giving the uninsured security in case of a tragedy, this would spread the cost of medical care out more equitably so that health insurance companies wouldn't be shouldering so much of the burden.

Another overlooked danger of the current system is what happens when there is a major epidemic or pandemic such as the often mentioned bird flu. In that situation, you would have thousands of uninsured people flooding the hospitals in search of treatment. The result is hospitals having to figure out a way of averting a financial crisis and going bankrupt rather than being able to focus all their resources on the health crisis. While the government would eventually step in and bail out our hospitals, it is irresponsible to not create mechanisms to safeguard the financial integrity of our health care system. The danger is that we run the risk of depending on a quick government response when it is not prepared to handle the task, much like the situation with hurricane Katrina.

Some states are already making moves to mandate universal health insurance. Other states are cautiously waiting to see what works before they make such a commitment. I commend the politicians that are trying to make something happen for their people in that regard, since that is what having authority is for.

One of the problems politicians will face is how functional their plans for state health insurance will be in relation to the current dynamics of how health insurance is currently paid for, and how the new plan might impact that. For example, will employers cut wages or jobs because of the new requirements to pay for health insurance? If a cheaper state health insurance plan is offered for employers to cover workers, will some employers who currently provide more expensive coverage switch to the cheaper plan? What will be the health insurance industry's reaction to that development? These are legitimate questions and that's why it would be best to start with a more limited emergency health care coverage plan. Politicians need to be aware that if you bite off more than you can chew, not only will you pay a political price, but you might set back your state from addressing the health care dilemma.

Once the Emergency Medical Care Fund is in place, there will be expectations for hospitals to stop overcharging those who have health insurance. The health insurance industry should then pass on those savings to American taxpayers and businesses. The free market system can only work if these institutions are honest about these cuts in cost. If not, our society will then have to seriously consider nationalizing health care. That's a worst case scenario however, and I'm willing to assume that with a fair system in place, hospitals and health insurance companies will act with integrity.

As long as our government is unwilling to take the responsibility of figuring out a way to pay the cost of emergency health care for the uninsured, the costs will continue to be shifted onto those with insurance. The corruption of this scheme has been eating away at our economy for some time now. As a society, we must share our burdens and that's what the Emergency Medical Care Fund will help accomplish.

SOLAR FUND

As the world's population continues to grow and non-renewable resources are stretched to their maximum output, we are beginning to make the shift to cleaner forms of renewable energy. Clearly, there is a lot of work to be done and it is especially hard in economies whose infrastructures are based on the use of non-renewable resources that create so much pollution. One of the problems with the Kyoto Protocol, was the economic impact that would result from agreeing to mandate those required changes in energy use. It was unrealistic that all the signatories would comply, and that would bring up the issue of who would be in charge of monitoring and enforcing Kyoto. Furthermore, big business interests that would lose money would certainly punish politicians that agreed to impose these regulations.

Knowing how the political process works, both abroad and in the U.S.A., the failure to adopt Kyoto could still be turned into a positive result. Let's assume for a moment that we do have a free press. If the press motivates consumers to pressure businesses to operate in a more energy efficient manner, that could reduce emissions with as much success as Kyoto would have. Have we no culture? Must we be forced to do what's right for ourselves and posterity by laws? This applies to individuals as well as corporations in their energy use. Global warming has received a lot of attention lately and as a society we're beginning to lean in the right direction. It's not enough to lean though, we have to start moving in that direction.

From the policy standpoint, there are still some things we can do. Concentrating Solar Power, or CSP, is the best use of solar technology available. It relies on hundreds of mirrors reflecting sunlight onto a tower, kind of like trying to burn something with a magnifying glass. The tower uses this heat to produce steam to power an electric turbine. This technology is already being used in Spain, and a new plant can generate enough electricity to supply a town of 6,000 people.

So, what is stopping this technology from being used to the degree that it cuts pollution and reduces demand for fossil fuels? If you look at a map, it's the poor countries that get most of the sunlight. The problem with solar technology is that the set-up with the mirrors is very expensive. The developed countries need to work together to make solar technology viable for developing countries.

As mentioned, one of the problems we face in the developed world, in changing our energy habits is that we have built our entire infrastructure around the use of fossil fuels. Therefore, it will be tremendously expensive to make the shift to cleaner forms of energy. In the developing world we have an opportunity to prevent countries that are still in the process of building their infrastructures from following our model. Since they are poor countries, once they are set up as fossil fuel based economies, it is very unlikely that they will have the ability to shift their energy habits because of the tremendous costs that would incur.

The big economies and polluters should create a Solar Fund specifically for subsidizing the building of these CSP plants in the developing world. The International Energy Agency, founded after the oil embargoes of the 1970's, could coordinate this program. The Solar Fund would select the most stable countries in the first wave of CSP building. These countries would have to offer land for the site, and make a request to the IEA for consideration in the program. The IEA would select countries in order of their ranking on how they protect human rights. The list would be made by the U.N. and revised every year, perhaps giving an incentive to rogue nations to straighten out their act if they want to get help. After building a CSP plant, the government would be given control of the plant with the agreement that they would charge ten percent less than the equivalent cost per megawatt from a conventional plant. Profits would go towards maintaining that plant and investing in more solar energy. In a large country, this could go to building more CSP plants. In a smaller country, where land might be scarce, the money could go towards putting solar panels on buildings. Because a degree of trust will be necessary, we should focus on helping governments that, although poor, are not corrupt.

Cutting the cost of energy by ten percent will provide an incentive to switch to solar power and free up money for development in other areas. These are poor countries and for the government, businesses and individuals to save ten percent on energy will make a big difference on everyone's bottom line. Obviously, any time we can do something to change the dynamics that are a factor in causing poverty, we should attempt to do so. In some poorer countries, it would make sense to charge even less for solar energy, and have a percentage of the profits go directly into fighting poverty. Each government's situation should be looked at, on a case by case scenario before determining what kind of agreement the IEA wants from them. We've found out all too often, over the years, that sanctions don't work very well. Perhaps rewarding good governments will be more effective than punishing bad ones, in motivating change.

Funding for this program would come from developed nations, where the use of this technology is not as feasible. Rather than a developed nation focusing solely on cutting their own pollution, they could pay money to the Solar Fund that would count towards decreasing worldwide pollution. The more a country pollutes, the more they should contribute. On top of developed nations agreeing to do this, charitable contributions could come from individuals and corporations. There's no reason why we can't have CSP plants all over Central America, North Africa, and Southeast Asia, in the next five years. We should also be able to get plants in small islands across the South Pacific and Caribbean. Since rising water levels due to global warming will impact these countries the most, you can be sure they'd all love switching to solar power as soon as possible.

From an economic standpoint, if developing nations in the tropics can reduce their use of coal and oil, the price of these commodities will drop. The decrease of use will also lengthen the amount of time it will take to deplete our non-renewable resources. Making coal and oil cheaper and longer lasting would, over time, make the Solar Fund pay for itself.

The initial cut in cost wouldn't be very big because the poor countries only consume a fraction of these resources on the world market. Yet, even the slightest fraction adds up quite significantly when you're talking about billions of barrels of oil. Let's say this program is put into effect for two years, and the corresponding effect is only a .50¢ drop in the cost of a barrel of oil. If we were to continue on that pattern, every two years, the developed countries would recoup billions of dollars on their investment in CSP projects. This is one of the rare win-win situations you will find in dealing with the world's energy problems.

Further investments could be made by developed countries in developing public and private transportation that runs on electricity in poorer countries. For example, major cities currently suffering from traffic congestion would greatly benefit from adding a fleet of electric buses or trains. While this is very expensive, it can happen with some creativity, especially since governments of developing nations could provide a large percentage of the funds for the project. If you're running a government and you can get electric rail in your city at two thirds of the cost of what it would normally be, you can't pass up that opportunity. The World Bank could provide loans, if necessary, to make it happen. Development costs money, and just like everywhere else, the government has to be willing to spend some money. The smarter governments in the developing world will understand the opportunity offered and get in on the deal.

As to private transportation, the cost of an electric automobile is simply too expensive for most people in the developing world at this time. However, the electric motorcycle is within the realm of possibility for many of these people, even though they are more expensive than the gas powered motorcycles of the same quality. However, the savings on gasoline over the lifetime of the motorcycle would make up for the difference in cost. An added bonus is that utility companies would have a steady demand for energy throughout the evening, as people re-charged their bikes, which would cause the overall price of electricity to go down. Promoting the sales of these vehicles would not be difficult if there was the will to do it. Tax breaks, low down payments and interest rates, advertising subsidies, etc…, would make things happen quicker.

Developing countries need to accept that global warming will require global cooperation in implementing solutions. After rejecting Kyoto, President George W. Bush has demonstrated a complete failure in imagination by not proposing some alternative solution to address global warming as a global community. The Solar Fund is more pro-active than Kyoto and helps developing countries avoid following in the footsteps of our energy consumption habits. Making it affordable for developing nations to buy into the technology should be a no brainer. Making capital available to do this is what will separate governments serious about solving the world's problems from those simply willing to provide lip service.

WINDOWS OF OPPORTUNITY

During the 1990's, America was blessed with a great opportunity to address a number of social problems. What made this possible was the booming economy that gave states and the Federal Government the ability to spend more, while maintaining a balanced budget. The main problem the government attempted to address was crime, and much of the surplus tax revenue went to adding police and building prisons.

One lesson taught in economics classes is that when you purchase one item, it costs you the opportunity of using that same money to buy something else. This is called an opportunity cost and it shows that every financial decision has multiple implications. What could our government have possibly done for our society that was better than adding cops and prisons? What has that policy cost us in lost opportunities?

Most of our social problems could have been addressed by fully funding higher education, or at least providing interest free loans, so that every American that graduates high school could go to college or technical school. Obviously, they would have to be accepted somewhere, but money should not be an obstacle preventing any American from higher education.

Under the current educational system, the government already subsidizes the majority of universities in this country. Some taxpayers can not afford to send their children to these universities however. What kind of democracy is that? The poor pay taxes to subsidize the college education of the wealthy, while hoping for scholarships or grants to get in! Why should the poor have to beg for scraps from the table like dogs? As taxpayers and citizens in a democracy, their seat at the table should be no different than anyone else's.

People from all over the world come to the United States to go to college. Yet we have families who for generations, have paid taxes that have gone into supporting our university systems, but not one member of their family has ever been able to go to college. This is a national tragedy. As it is, the cost of putting someone through college is barely affordable for the middle class.

Imagine living in a society where children are told that they can become anything they want to, and it's actually true? Do you think that the children of the poor believe America is that type of country? The high crime rates in poor communities show that many juveniles feel there is no hope in their future. What else can explain such self-destructive behavior?

What would happen if poor children knew that if they stayed in school, and stayed away from drugs, they could actually obtain the knowledge that would give them the opportunity to become anything. That would be a social experiment worth trying. Today, we have public service messages saying "Stay in School," but what they really mean is, "Stay in school, as long as you can afford it."

Another benefit of a free education is if people don't have to spend so much to become a doctor, then they no longer have to demand such a high salary to pay back the money they owe for their education. In the long run, we end up paying for everyone's education anyway, plus interest on the loans. So, who profits from the current system? Financial institutions who make the loans.

In fairness, this system is an overall reflection of the way Americans conduct their personal business. Take the way Americans waste so much gasoline as an example. Only when America is on the verge of crisis, would Americans consider buying more fuel efficient vehicles. No, I'm not talking about the crisis of global warming. That's not even happening according to many Americans. When gasoline got to three dollars a gallon, Americans began rethinking their modes of transportation.

There are some people who have to drive SUVs or pick-ups because they have a business or six children that make using such vehicles practical. These people are in fact victims of the rest of those Americans who selfishly buy gas guzzling chariots to satisfy some superficial whim. Anyone who pays taxes is also a victim of this wasteful behavior.

When gas prices go up because of greater demand, our government takes the biggest hit. The cost of services increases for school buses, snow plows, garbage trucks and all military vehicles, all police and sheriff's vehicles, the postal service, and the list goes on and on. You'd think as much as people whine about how high their taxes are in this country, they'd try to cut the cost of government by buying a more efficient vehicle. Every police and sheriff's department should be required to purchase automobiles that get better than forty miles per gallon. If Toyota makes a fortune, so what? Every new taxi added by existing companies should also have to get forty miles per gallon. That's just a start. Americans need to wake up and understand the opportunity costs of their wasteful energy habits.

If we want our government to become efficient, then we have to adopt the same attitude.

The wastefulness and inefficiency in the way America handles energy, education and crime, are things that we can do something about, right now. The longer we procrastinate, the more dire the consequences. The energy issue has obvious environmental and economic consequences. Education and crime are linked and addressing educational inequalities will reduce crime.

A lot of what you see on TV about crime, especially in regards to gangs, started in the penitentiary. While some gangs were born in prisons, others have direct prison influences. People might not see the correlation between what's going on in the streets and prisons, but there is a connection. All these tough on crime advocates must remember that it will come out on the street some day.

While I am able to explain the problems of the legal system, there are many who can't. Imagine the frustration and anger convicts feel while trying to explain what is wrong with the system, but simply can't find the right words. Where does that lead?

The bitterness and resentment in our prisons have been building for some time now. Throwing someone's life away as though it were trash, for political gain, is a dangerous example. Using hate in our dialogue about criminals can only lead to hate for government being reciprocated. Hate combined with frustration results in irrational acts.

Just like on September 11th, when many Americans found out how much our government was hated overseas, it will probably be some radical, outrageous act that awakens Americans to the fury growing every day in our prison system. When that happens, the threat from Al Qaeda will look tame.

Changing the system into a legal justice system would be a step in the right direction, but that would only impact the people coming into the system. We've already got over two million people locked up and there is no relief in sight. States with large prison populations should set up commissions to review cases and make recommendations to the governor for sentence commutations. It's better to do this before prison overcrowding gets so out of hand that a state is forced to release prisoners without any thorough review. While it looks better for politicians to claim they were forced to release prisoners, leaders should deal with this problem while it is still manageable.

The cost of incarceration is often measured at between thirty and thirty-five thousand dollars per year, per inmate. This is a false measurement. Those prisoners that could hold down a job and function in society, would pay an additional twenty to twenty-five thousand dollars a year in income and other taxes. You could say this is true of at least ten percent of our two million plus prisoners. Then there is the immeasurable cost of these prisoners not being there for their children, parents and grandparents. How does this affect the lives of all those parties, and the way they perceive a government so willing to deprive them of their loved ones for prison terms that often don't make any sense. You wonder why hatred towards authority is so ingrained in certain parts of our society? In many cases they have no way of knowing just when that person will be released. Dad could be home next year, or in ten years, depending on the Parole Board. It should be noted that most of prisoners' children in the present system end up becoming involved in the prison system.

This isn't a game like cops and robbers. People die when this system doesn't work. We live in a society that has been led to believe that the answers are real simple. Build more prisons, add more cops, pass more laws. I hope that after reading these essays, people will understand just how complicated things really are. We live in the 21st century. If leaders continue to dumb down our problems to fit political slogans, or thirty second commercials, we will not solve anything.

There is a lot at stake here. The world will continue to become more complicated and we are at risk of not being up to the challenge. Despite everything, America is still in a prime position to change the world. The resources are there. Will the next generation have the initiative to get it done? Will misguided leaders keep Americans from getting through the window of opportunity before it shuts? I hope that America, like a crack addict, doesn't have to hit rock bottom before it begins its course to recovery.

BIBLIOGRAPHY

Part I

Mann, Horace, *Thoughts On Wisdom*. Forbes Inc., 1995.

Culture

Solzhenitsyn, Alexandr, *The Gulag Archipelago Two*. Harper & Row, Publishers. ISBN 0-06-08-345-2. (pbk)

Helvetius, *Les Philosophes*, p.189.

Dostoevski, Fedor, from the preface of *Crusaders, Criminals, Crazies*, by Dr. Frederick Hacker. Bantam Books.

Multiculturalism

Lewis, C.S. *Mere Christianity*. MacMillan Publishing Co, p.74. Library of Congress, catalog card No. 81-12339.

Diderot, Denis, *From Dawn to Decadence,* by Jacques Barzun. Harper Collins Publishers, 2000.

The Legal Political System

Adams. John Quincy, *Profiles In Courage*, by John F. Kennedy. Harper Collins.

Who watches over government

Montesquieu, Charles de Secondat, Baron de la Brede et de, *The Western Intellectual Tradition* by J. Bronowski & Bruce Mazlish. Harper Torchbooks, 1975. ISBN 0-06-133001-9.

Fénelon, François de Salignac de La Mothe, *From Dawn to Decadence*, by Jacques Barzun. Harper Collins Publishers, 2000.

Leviathan

Hobbes, Thomas, *The Western Intellectual Tradition*, by J. Bronowski & Bruce Mazlish. Harper Torchbooks,1975. ISBN 0-06-133001-9.

Juvenile Suffrage

Travisono, Anyhony P., *Corrections in America*. McMillan Publishing Company, 1992. ISBN 0-02-301725-2

Rehabilitation

Tocqueville, Alexis de, *Democracy In America*. Schoken Books, Fifth Printing, 1972. Library of Congress, Catalog No. 61-16651.

Montesquieu, *Les philosophes*.

Corrections in America. McMillan Publishing Company, 1992. ISBN 0-02-301725-2

Designing A Legal Justice System

Freedman, Eric M., from *"The Life Preserver"*, by James Traub. The New Yorker, April 8, 1996, p.47.

Porter, Everette M., *Corrections In America*. MacMillan Publishing Company, 1992. ISBN 0-02-301725-2.

Part II

Mill, John Stuart, *On Liberty*. London, 1859.

Understanding Iraq

De Gaulle, Charles, *Vietnam, The Decisive Battles*, by John Pimlott. Marshall Editions, 1997. London, p.24. ISBN 0-78581760-3.

War Strategy

D'Abernon, Lord, *God's Playground: A History of Poland II*, by Norman Davies. Columbia University Press, 2005, p. 297. ISBN 0231128193.

The Bible and Science

Erasmus, Desiderius, *From Dawn to Decadence,* by Jacques Barzun. Harper Collins Publishers, 2000.

.

www.ingramcontent.com/pod-product-compliance
Lightning Source LLC
Chambersburg PA
CBHW051429280526
45785CB00003B/1218